Egypt Inside Out

Egypt Inside Out

Trevor Naylor

Photographs by
Doriana Dimitrova

The American University in Cairo Press
Cairo • New York

First published in 2020 by
The American University in Cairo Press
113 Sharia Kasr el Aini, Cairo, Egypt
200 Park Ave., Suite 1700, New York, NY 10166
www.aucpress.com

Dar el Kutub No. 13062/18
ISBN 978 977 416 904 5

Dar el Kutub Cataloging-in-Publication Data

Naylor, Trevor
    Egypt Inside Out / Trevor Naylor.—Cairo: The American University in Cairo Press, 2020.
    p.   cm.
    ISBN: 978 977 416 904 5
    Egypt—History—21st Century
    I. Title
    916.2

1 2 3 4 5   24 23 22 21 20

Designed by Fatiha Bouzidi
Printed in China

For the ninety-six.
You will never walk alone.

Contents

Acknowledgments

It may be said of some very old places, as of some very old books, that they are destined to be forever new. The nearer we approach them, the more remote they seem; the more we study them, the more we have yet to learn. Time augments rather than diminishes their everlasting novelty; and to our descendants of a thousand years hence it may safely be predicted that they will be even more fascinating than to ourselves. This is true of many ancient lands, but of no place is it so true as of Egypt.

—Amelia B. Edwards, *Pharaohs, Fellahs and Explorers*, 1891

Trevor—This book took longer than expected, which means more people to thank. Everyone who follows helped in a real way to get me over the line: Narisa Chakrabongse, Doriana Dimitrova, Miriam Fahmi, Nigel Fletcher-Jones, Ehab and Manal Gaddis, Emad Iskander, Shahat Shaheto, Tayea Ismail, Emam Sabry Khalil, Sameh el-Moghazy, Ester Nader, Nadia Naqib, Cherif Samaan, Ingrid Wassmann, and many more people across Egypt and farther afield, including my family, who have waited patiently.

Doriana—My journey through Egypt recording life and landscapes has been achieved with the love and support of Philip Warren, whom I met and married during the same time. I thank him for being there to see Egypt through my eyes and enjoying it just as much through my memories.

Introduction

Aesthetic expression does not come from just what the eye sees, but from everything one feels, clearly or confusedly.
—Ramses Wissa Wassef, *Woven by Hand*, 1972

If I were to identify the moment when I really fell in love with Egypt, I would have to choose January 6, 1989. I had been in Cairo for one and a half years. It was my first time living outside England and my first experience of a foreign culture. I was having fun, I had made friends, and I was newly single. However, I was still, ultimately, a stranger in a strange land. It took an event to connect me to Egypt and make me part of its national psyche.

The event was a football match between Egypt and Liberia. Unbeknownst to my friends, I was most excited about seeing George Weah, the dynamic young footballer who had recently joined Monaco Football Club and, at the time of writing, is president of Liberia. I had heard of Weah, but was unaware of any Egyptian football stars. How things changed that night when, in front of fifty thousand Egyptians, the "Pharaohs" of football beat Liberia two goals to nil.

I was hooked. It was the first international football match I had seen and, as I followed Egypt's path to qualification for the 1990 World Cup in Italy, I began a journey that was to carry me ever deeper inside my adopted home.

Egypt at that time was already crowded, and is becoming ever more so. Walking through some parts of Cairo has a chaotic intensity, with noise, pollution, and everyone rushing to his or her destination. In contrast, a football crowd has an intensity born of focused proximity. Unlike the daily competitive struggle of millions of poorer Egyptians, at a match the

Emerging from a hot tomb visit to a cool breeze, here in the Valley of the Queens

crowd is as one and their support is vociferous. The crowd *needs* Egypt to win.

I came away from that evening feeling I knew far more about the multilayered society in which I was privileged to live. I began to wonder if this country I'd grown to love was often misunderstood by those who passed through. I had begun to write a book . . . in my head.

Many years later, that book was published. *Cairo Inside Out* provided glimpses of the city I had lived in and visited for thirty years. I revisited and illustrated those places that most resonated in my memory, that I wanted to share with those visiting Egypt today. The book was well received and generated reflections and favorable comments, from both first-time travelers and long-time residents.

Soon, however, calls started to arrive from friends in Luxor, Aswan, and Alexandria. "What about our city?" they said. Their prodding was the genesis of *Egypt Inside Out*.

As with *Cairo Inside Out*, this book attempts to capture the feel of Egypt through a combination of words and photographs. My long relationship with the country provides a map of experience upon which many of the cities and sites in the volume are marked. Many locations are interwoven with personal and family memories. Doriana's challenge was to capture the places, the light, and the sense of time I remembered. Her skill, keen eye, and ability to bring those around her into her pictures has succeeded in showcasing Egypt, creating a book that I hope is fresh, and distinct from the multitude of travel books that have preceded it.

The visual and human range of this book make it very different from *Cairo Inside Out*. Traveling the length and breadth of the country—down the Nile, through deserts, along the coast, in every type of transport and with the help of so many Egyptians—provided the base upon which this book

Abu Simbel's walls are rich in storytelling

was built. During our journeys, Doriana and I sat in countless places across Egypt, eating and chatting with people of all ages and from all backgrounds about their hopes and dreams, and their thoughts about their country and the world beyond.

Egypt has always been known for its special geography, its hospitable and humorous people, and its unique millennia-long history, a combination that ensures the country is a perennial travelers' favorite. *Egypt Inside Out* follows the Nile from Abu Simbel to the Mediterranean, and is intended to give the reader a new look at a classic journey. Revisiting the places I had been to many times before revived many happy moments from my life. I hope Doriana's photographs and my words convey some of those moments, and that the book will be enjoyed by both first-time visitors and those who have visited some of the places depicted and have a heartfelt connection to one of the world's great countries.

As one journeys farther from Cairo, the variety of ways in which you can choose to travel widens: cars, jeeps, taxis, airplanes, trains, horse-drawn carriages, tuk-tuks, small boats, and trams were all used during the writing of this book. During our travels, we met many people, both those from my past and new friends who embraced us and the project. It reminded me how proud Egyptians are of their country. At every level of society, people are keen to share whatever they have with their guests. It has always been my experience in Egypt that those with the least to give are the most generous. Over and over, we were invited by people we had just met to share food and drink, or were given the finest treatment. Though it is sometimes humbling, I have learned to go with the flow and enjoy sharing a few minutes together and breaking bread with Egyptians I've never met before. This is all part of knowing Egypt Inside Out, and is what has made writing the book so enjoyable. Egypt is a land of smiles . . . and increasingly of selfies. This modern form of making friends goes a long way when language is a barrier. Say yes to sharing in a selfie, and take one yourself, and you will start to make friends.

Don't forget to look around you. My hope is that this book will inspire you to find the special sense of place that Egypt can impart, and that you will give yourself time for the country to touch your soul. Egypt is there for you to discover, visit slowly, learn its intricacies, and above all enjoy the vast bounty of its treasures.

Ramesses II built Abu Simbel to impress and
frighten his enemies. It still works today.

Aswan—Gateway to Egypt

For many centuries, Aswan's gentle pace and calm atmosphere have been part of its allure for visitors from Egypt and beyond. Arriving from any direction, by whatever means of transport, visitors will feel their cares falling away when they catch their first glimpse of the Nile at Aswan. Much of Egypt is under the strain of a swelling population, and Aswan is no exception. However, for now at least, Aswan seems to be absorbing its growth without losing its special sense of place, created by the contrast between the ancient sites of Philae and Abu Simbel and the twentieth-century technological achievement of the Aswan High Dam, set against the dramatic colors of blue sky, orange desert, and green trees.

Since ancient times, when it was known as Swenet, Aswan has been regarded as the gateway between Egypt and Africa. Like all gateway towns and border areas, it encourages visitors to wonder what lies beyond, in this case to the south, but on our journey to discover Egypt Inside Out we will travel north through the country, following the Nile on its route to the sea.

Perhaps your arrival in Aswan will have been preceded by the excitement of a visit to Abu Simbel or a cruise on Lake Nasser. Abu Simbel is arguably the second most prominent attraction in Egypt, after the Pyramids. The Abu Simbel site comprises two sacred temples built into a mountainside overlooking Lake Nasser. They dominate the skyline, and unlike many tourist experiences, they are genuinely awe-inspiring.

The temples were built during the reign of Pharaoh Ramesses II to celebrate his victory over the Hittites in the Battle of Kadesh in 1275 BC. They were originally sixty meters

Nubians are welcoming people,
in their homes and with their smiles

Simple and colorful art is part of Nubia's joyful appeal

below their current position, but were relocated by a huge UNESCO operation in 1969 to prevent them from being submerged after the construction of the Aswan High Dam. The temples at Abu Simbel are now located at the apex of an artificial cliff on Lake Nasser's western banks, some three hundred kilometers southwest of the dam.

The Egyptian government, in partnership with UNESCO, managed this over a period of four years, actually cutting the temple into pieces and moving it like a huge jigsaw puzzle. They achieved a minor miracle, with the result that subsequent generations have been able to enjoy the site. Photography is not allowed in the temples, which is a boon, because it forces you to fully appreciate the decoration, the architecture, and the amazing light cast by the doorways.

A boat trip from Aswan to Nubian villages is
an essential part of your relaxing visit

Looking out from these spaces is truly memorable, and perhaps as close as you can get to time travel in this ancient land.

For a very different visual and human experience, try a relaxing cruise on Lake Nasser. The views are breathtaking, and at night the skies are alive with stars. Should you want to try to catch a Nile perch, the small boats also offer great fishing.

The vast area that is now Lake Nasser was previously part of Nubia, home to the Nubian people of Sudan and Egypt. Modern Aswan lies along the Nile and around the shores of the lake. Here live the new generations of a culture that was largely submerged by the creation of the lake and the displacement of the Nubian peoples. Lake Nasser is now a vast reservoir some 550 kilometers long and up to 35 kilometers wide, making it one of the largest human-made lakes in the world.

Nubia was one of the earliest civilizations in Africa, with a history traceable to at least 2500 BC. It was home to several empires, most prominently the kingdom of Kush, which for nearly a century ruled Egypt itself.

The descendants of the ancient Nubians, relocated as the High Dam was built and the lake slowly filled, are the parents and grandparents of much of Aswan's population. Today they work in traditional roles as farmers, or in the lucrative tourism industry. It is estimated that some fifty thousand Nubians left the area to work in other parts of Egypt. Indeed, for many families in Aswan, the money sent by their extended family is a major source of income. Nubian culture has always been built on close family ties and pride in their unique ethnicity. This sense of difference pervades one's experience as a visitor to this uniquely beautiful place.

For another experience to remember, explore by boat the waters between the original Aswan Dam (built by the British between 1899 and 1902) and the High Dam (completed in 1970). Ideally, find a Nubian boatman to guide you along the shore an hour or two before sunset, when the interplay of sunlight and shade is magical. The soft chugging of the boat engine or the near silence of a felucca provides a gentle accompaniment to the passing landscape.

Aswan has been loved by European travelers since the time of Amelia Edwards, who visited Egypt in 1873–74 with friends. In Cairo they hired a traditional *dahabiya* houseboat and

The connection of sand, river, and sunset is a breathtaking sight unique to Aswan

Wherever you sit in Aswan,
a cat will be watching from somewhere

Crocodiles no longer live in the Nile below the
High Dam, but their history as animals and gods
in the past is still part of Nubian folklore

Islands in the Nile at Aswan offer beautiful settings for eating

traveled south, staying in the area of Philae and Abu Simbel for six weeks. Edwards wrote a vivid description of her Nile voyage, entitled *A Thousand Miles Up the Nile* (1877). Enhanced with her own illustrations, this early example of travel writing was an immediate best seller and remains readable and relevant today.

The challenge of writing today about such a place is to attempt to reflect the sensations that arise while passing through a truly ancient landscape and sensing the ghosts of the many who have passed through the place before you. The huge granite boulders and sweeping desert horizons of Aswan do not make you feel small; rather, they make you feel part of a vaster world.

Many visitors arrive in Aswan via a Nile cruise from Luxor. Although we have started our tour in Aswan, relaxing here after the bustle and hassle of the tourist sites of Luxor and the necropolis on its western shore may be the best approach. In Aswan, the slow pace of life is a result of the thousands of years of punishing summer heat. The need to conserve energy and protect oneself from the sun leads one to find refuges in which to relax and watch the Aswan days drift by.

Local children explore their river and have fun

River taxis pepper the waterside throughout Aswan

You do not need to be told to smile, but it helps

The lake trip between the two dams allows time to stop and meet the people who live on and from these waters. Villages that maintain the ancient Nubian culture have sprung up and welcome travelers from across the world.

If you wish to visit a Nubian village, there are two on Elephantine Island—Siou and Koti. They are connected by a short walk and feel almost like a single community. Many of the inhabitants are the direct descendants of those who were moved when the High Dam was built. Today it is a place where tourism and the modern world sit side by side with ancient Nubia, the villagers relying on visitors both for income and to help maintain their Nubian culture, architecture, art, clothing, music, food, and drink. There also several archaeological sites, which show that the island has been occupied since Predynastic times. In ancient Egypt, locals believed the island was inhabited by Khnum, the ram-headed god who controlled the waters of the Nile. According to tradition, Khnum molded humans from clay, and he is often depicted at his potter's wheel.

An essential part of any Aswan day is enjoying the local cuisine. There are plenty of choices if you wish to eat in one of the larger hotels, all of which offer great views. If you want to be more adventurous, try a mid-river dining experience, which comes with a boat trip, lovely decor, and Egyptian home-style dishes with, for once, lots to offer the vegetarian.

Nubian cuisine has been swept up under the general heading of Egyptian food. However, there are many traditional dishes to try in the area. The earliest evidence of ancient Nubian food was uncovered in the archaeology of Kerma, in Sudan. This important site revealed in its bakeries and ovens the first evidence of bread-making, which is integral to all Nubian meals. The best-known bread today, *kabed*, is much admired for its refined flavor. As it leaves the oven, it receives a sweet or savory filling. Eating *kabed* in Aswan with local people is a treat indeed.

Modern, well-equipped hotel villages are available for the budget traveler, here close to Philae Temple

Though Nubian culture was forced to change when Lake Nasser flooded the historical lands, the new generation has a strong drive to maintain the old traditions. Preserving one's food is to preserve one's history, and this is a process that begins in the home.

In these villages, families summon rich flavors from plants they grow in gardens along the Nile. Spices and oils are artfully added to okra, zucchini, spinach, peas, beans, and carrots to create mouthwatering dishes. Nubians also use meat, chicken, and fish in recipes that have been passed from generation to generation and are cooked in the simple, often mud-built, kitchens of their homes.

El Dokka is a traditional Nubian-style restaurant on one of the small islands near the First Cataract of the Nile, in front of the world-famous Old Cataract Hotel. Part of its charm is that it can only be reached by boat. You can eat inside or out, with achingly gorgeous vistas in all directions. In keeping with the pace of life in Aswan, you can sit as long as you wish before ordering; when you have ordered, the food will arrive in its own good time. The hearty local Egyptian cuisine does plenty to encourage an afternoon or after-dinner nap, though to get to your bed you will need to flag down another felucca or boat.

These popular tourist figures can be bought while you wait for your boat trip around the lake

Inside Out—Egyptian food and Nubian landscape

Places to sit in the shade and take tea provide a refreshing break before the boat ride back to Aswan

El Dokka restaurant in Aswan has modern design and traditional food

Arriving at Philae on the island
of Agilkia is always a thrill

Cats often steal the best sunbathing spots,
but add life to ancient history

Ancient windows on the modern world—Philae Temple

Boats are integral to Aswan. If you stay a few days, it is likely you'll spend more time in them than in a taxi or car. Indeed, this is one of the ways this remote city enters your soul and slows you down. Surveying the Nile from its banks and seeing it from water level are two very different experiences. One of the most vital boat rides is the short but pleasurable crossing to Philae Island. Sharing the motorboats can be fun, and on a busy day you will almost certainly have to do so. However, it is worth paying a little more and asking the driver to take you farther out into the lake and around its small islands. The view back toward the first dam and the 360-degree panorama are additional treats en route to one of ancient Egypt's finest treasures.

Philae Temple and its surrounding buildings are by any standard a miracle of survival. Philae was one of the last outposts of Egyptian religion, surviving two centuries after the Roman Empire converted to Christianity. This sacred island attracted many Greek and Roman pilgrims, who came to make offerings and pray to the Egyptian goddess Isis.

Tea in the temple

Philae Temple has been an important
site for many of Egypt's pharaohs and
conquerors

This special view from Philae is one of Egypt's finest Inside Out panoramas,
a place where it is easy to imagine our ancestors enjoying the sunrise in this beautiful land

Glimpses of Nubia from the Temple of Isis

The earliest building was a small temple dedicated to Isis around 370 BC, which was enlarged over time by subsequent rulers to become the stunning Temple of Isis. Ptolemy II (285–246 BC) began the real expansion of the temple, with another major building campaign undertaken six hundred years later by the Roman emperor Diocletian (r. AD 284–305). The temples continued to be a popular destination for religious visitors until they were finally closed in AD 535 by order of Emperor Justinian. Nevertheless, through adaptation, the buildings survived and some of the smaller temples became Christian sites. A Coptic community moved to the island and lived there until the coming of Islam to the region in the seventh century. Like so much of Nubia, its treasures were neglected for a millennium until the beginning of tourism from Europe in the eighteenth and nineteenth centuries, when Philae again became a popular destination. Then, at the beginning of the twentieth century, its real survival test began. With the building of the first Aswan Dam, the island became submerged for much of the year, making visits difficult and damaging the lower parts of the temples.

Philae would have been submerged by the rising water below the High Dam, but was rescued by the huge UNESCO Nubian Monuments project, which took place between 1972 and 1980. In order to save the Philae monuments, the original island was surrounded by a dam and drained. On the nearby island of Agilkia, a new site was made ready to host the monuments. The temples were broken into many numbered sections. They were then painstakingly reerected on Agilkia in as close an arrangement and alignment as possible to their original positions. Philae lived on. This architectural miracle is well worth remembering as you look out from the majestic site through the many windows and doors, which reveal stunning vistas in every direction.

In Philae there are many spots to sit and read in a shady corner or in the quaintly positioned café and shop, nestling under trees with a dazzling view. I chose a quiet corner under a tree to revisit my copy of *Baedeker's Egypt and the Sudan* (1908). This tome, though turgidly written, remains accurate and useful. The author tells us that before the temples of Philae were moved, the original island was known as El-Kasr, or Geziret Anas el Wogud. This was based on the hero of a tale from the *Thousand and One Nights* adapted to an Egyptian setting. The story was related by boatmen to visitors of the time as follows: Once upon a time, there was a king who had a handsome favorite named Anas el Wogud and a vizier who had a beautiful daughter named Zahr el-Ward (Flower of the Rose). These two young people fell in love and met secretly until they were discovered. The vizier was furious, and to keep his daughter safe he banished her to Philae Island, where she was imprisoned in the Temple of Isis. Despite her

disappearance, her young lover could not forget her and wandered far and wide hoping to see her once more. As he traveled through deserts and elsewhere, he showed acts of kindness and made friends with many animals. One day a hermit told him that his love was locked on the island, and so he made his way to the bank to cross the water. The water was full of crocodiles, but one of the dangerous beasts decided to carry him safely across as thanks for his past kindness to animals. When he arrived, many birds came to tell him that Zahr el-Ward was on the island. However, he could not find her, as she in turn, out of desperation to find him, had escaped using a rope made of her clothes and found a shipmaster to carry her away. The long romantic tale ends when the two finally meet after months of searching and the girl's father agrees to their marriage.

It is easy to imagine such a tale being spun to visitors over a century ago as they saw the Temple of Isis on the horizon from their boat. Philae also offers a beautiful sound-and-light show that illuminates both the temple and the sky above and is well worth the extra trip out at night.

Aswan's main street is one long bazaar,
with goods of the past and the present

some of the hassle-driven areas in Cairo and around the main sites. That said, remember to always bargain hard, and be prepared to walk away. The author William Golding wrote: "He who rides the sea of the Nile must have sails woven of patience," and, while sitting and watching the interplay of visitors and storekeepers in Aswan market, I could imagine he had just been shopping when he wrote those words. A visit to the bazaar in late afternoon is suffused with beams of light while providing much-needed shade. Take time to savor the atmosphere, recognizing that every street has its own story waiting to be discovered.

A more compact place to shop is the short street of stores at the site of the unfinished obelisk. Here is the best bookshop in Aswan, stocking a range of books to answer most of your questions about ancient Egypt. And be sure to stop by the weavers making scarves on traditional looms. The shaded walk provides a good opportunity to linger, catch one's breath, and savor a cool drink.

This archaeological site is in the full glare of the sun, but is particularly fascinating as it reveals how these huge monuments were carved from solid granite before being raised and moved to their final sites. This example, if finished, would have been the largest ever made, over forty meters tall. During the work, commissioned by Queen Hatshepsut some 3,500 years ago, cracks appeared in the stone and the project was abandoned. The unfinished obelisk offers unique insights into ancient Egyptian stoneworking techniques, with the marks from the workers' tools still clearly visible as well as lines indicating where they were working. To stand there in the suffocating daytime heat is to understand the ancient Egyptian devotion to duty, and to the gods and pharaohs.

While foreigners have been seeking inspiration from the great sites of Aswan for several centuries, in the last few years young Egyptians have been rediscovering their heritage. One factor has been the difficult economic times, which have led to a surge in domestic tourism. More recently, however, an Egyptian TV series based in Aswan kept the country

The tourist experience of Aswan is for many all too short, as the key sites are checked off the list and the coach or boat heads to the next destination. In such targeted travel, it is easy to lose track of the fact that you are in a functioning city. The markets of Aswan are vibrant, and at night are especially colorful places to shop and sit in the coffeehouses, where you may well enjoy a friendly encounter. While the stores on Shari' al-Suq sell tourist items, the streets around are for local shoppers, and this is a refreshing change from

Wandering through the souk in Aswan is fun. The mixture of local goods, local shoppers, and tourist trinkets makes for a pleasant time in shady streets.

The colors of the market extend to its visitors as well

enthralled during Ramadan and encouraged many younger Egyptians to make a visit.

The series, entitled *Grand Hotel*, is set in the 1950s. Ali, a young man, arrives at the grand hotel in the beautiful city of Aswan to investigate the disappearance of his younger sister. He gets a job as a waiter and falls in love with Nazly, the daughter of the owner. She sets out to help him to discover the truth about his sister's disappearance. Along the way, the story takes various twists and turns as it uncovers the mysteries behind the wonderful grand hotel. The combination of glamorous history, intrigue, and wonderful scenery evokes the era of Royal Egypt, which is enjoying a revival of interest among a new generation of Egyptians. Historically, the settings of great hotels such as the Old Cataract or Luxor's Winter Palace have been the backdrop for Western movies in which wealthy tourists and Egyptologists took pride of place. *Grand Hotel* represents an Egyptian reclaiming of this heritage.

The Old Cataract Hotel in Aswan is one of the grandest hotels in the country, and is a marvelous sanctuary for well-heeled refugees. Whether your budget allows for a cup of tea or a five-course dinner in one of its magnificent restaurants, the Old Cataract is a must-see. Countless famous names have graced the hotel since it was built for Thomas Cook as the host hotel for its high-class European cruise travelers in 1899.

Visitors to the Unfinished Obelisk site in Aswan have the chance to learn about Egypt's history at the Nubia Bookstore

Attractive models of Nubian life to take home after your trip

This weaver shows visitors the traditional ways of making Egypt's fine textiles on his loom

The view from the terrace is on the bucket list of many travelers, and it is easy to imagine sharing the tables and sofas there with Tsar Nicholas II, Winston Churchill, Jimmy Carter, Princess Diana, Queen Noor, the Shah of Iran, or François Mitterrand. With the filming of *Grand Hotel*, the hotel now proudly includes Amr Youssef, Amina Khalil, and Mohamed Mamdouh in its list of stars. Agatha Christie set part of *Death on the Nile* in this hotel, though it was written mostly in her Luxor hotel, the Winter Palace.

Looking out across the felucca-spotted Nile toward Elephantine Island at any time of day is a pleasure, and the sense of history is palpable.

Inside and out, the sheer proportions of the building epitomize grandeur, with art deco meeting Mamluk style in halls adorned with photographs of historic moments and famous visitors to the Old Cataract. There is a sense that you are traveling back in time to a more elegant era, as you

The Old Cataract Hotel has one of Egypt's finest
terraces for breakfast

Looking toward the
Cataract Hotel, the
classic postcard image
of Aswan

The Old Cararact Hotel Terrace—a place to share Egypt's recent history

wander beneath Moorish domes and Byzantine arches, and walk on Persian carpets.

For most visitors, of course, their choice of accommodation may not include this finest of venues, but Aswan does have many alternatives. Isis Island offers a resort nestled within extraordinary gardens, with boats available for any trip you wish to make. Breakfast is taken on the terrace surrounded by lush green gardens, the blue of the Nile, and the deep orange of the desert. Similarly, the hotels on Elephantine Island are havens of tranquility, with views to lift the spirits and relax the mind. Originally the military gatepost in the defense of Egypt, this sizable island is where Aswan began. Today it houses the Nubian villages and the modern Aswan Museum. It is also home to two of the three remaining Nilometers in Egypt, whose purpose was to record the rise and fall of the river during its annual inundation. The location of Elephantine Island was especially important: being at the gateway of Egypt, it was the first place where the beginning of the annual flood could be seen.

The corridors of the Old Cataract Hotel glisten under Moorish-influenced architecture

OPPOSITE: Recent renovations have brought the Cataract Hotel back to its glitzy, spectacular best

Every corner of this sumptous hotel incorporates
fine design and detail

Objects from across the Middle East
decorate the hotel

The arched Moorish interiors are
an iconic element of this hotel's
worldwide fame

The magnificent dining room is a grand place to celebrate good times (left). The skillful architects allowed enough light to showcase the interior, while maintaining a cool atmosphere (above)

FOLLOWING PAGES:
This level of grandeur is required when your guests include world royalty, presidents and prime ministers, celebrities and historical figures. The Old Cataract has hosted them all in fine style.

Elephantine Island in Aswan has both hotels and local villages side by side. It is a charming place to walk and its painted walls, interiors, and doorways provide splashes of color as you pass by. You will be welcomed everywhere, and coffee is always ready.

Wandering around Elephantine
Island may lead you past an informal
Nubian museum, a place that shows
you how local people live and
decorate their homes

Looking west from Elephantine Island the desert sands begin, glowing in the late evening sun
—a perfect time to enjoy the day's memories

Aswan is unique, and as you leave you may experience the regret that comes from saying goodbye to a truly unforgettable location. Part of its ability to thrill may stem from an otherworldliness created by distance, both in space and in time. Aswan days unfold from the placid dawns through the torpid heat of afternoon to late afternoon when beams of light shimmer through the trees and bounce off the concentric rings created by Nile fish as they surface or the many birds swooping to catch their evening meal.

A Train Ride

While a cruise between Aswan and Luxor is undoubtedly the perfect way to travel this route, a train from
one to the other provides a fascinating Inside-Out glimpse of Egyptian rural life and is highly recommended

Luxor—
The Ancient Past Inside Out

Luxor. The very name entices. In a world where any location is visually available online in seconds, this is one place that needs to be experienced in person to reveal its beauty and grandeur.

Luxor has had several names over the millennia. It was known as Waset in ancient Egyptian texts, and Thebes by the Greeks and then the Romans when it became an important spiritual center. Its current name, Luxor, is derived from the Arabic *al-Uqsur*, 'the palaces.'

Today the population is around half a million, but it is swelled during the year by the arrival of tourists. From November through March the weather is outstanding, and this, together with the historic sites, has drawn visitors to the area for centuries. In the blistering heat of May to August, Luxor is

Kings Island Luxor is a private resort area of long standing. A walk around its lovely gardens at first light can bring you to early mists and greenery before the heat of the day envelops you.

OPPOSITE: Looking across the Nile to balloons rising over the west bank at Luxor

asleep for much of the day, serving only the hardiest visitors, while the verdant fields are harvested in the early morning as the east and west banks of the Nile simmer in the burning sun.

Even in the cooler months, Upper Egypt merits the Inside Out approach. Indeed, your first sight will most likely be from your chosen mode of transport—usually the window of a plane or train. The train comes into Luxor from Cairo

The walkway to Queen Hapshetsut's temple provides shade, shopping, and a pattern to your approach

The Colossi of Memnon are representations of Amenhotep III. Always impressive, they seem to guard the treasures of the west bank of Luxor. They are often the new visitor's first encounter with ancient Egypt's massive statuary.

OPPOSITE: Recently renovated tombs in Luxor are like art galleries, with breathtaking paintings and atmospheric light

or Aswan, and the latter four-hour journey is a fine way to observe Egypt at ground level. A trip from Luxor to Aswan by boat and then a return by train makes an excellent itinerary. From the comfort of your train seat you can sip tea and watch rural Egypt unfold before you: farmers and animals working the landscape as they have done for millennia, trains transporting sugarcane, and donkey carts taking produce to market.

It may come as a shock to find that the Luxor tourist day begins before dawn. The many hotels, cruise boats, and tourist sites all start with the sun. For the locals it was ever thus, given that Luxor's life has been driven by the cycle of the river

and the seasonal harvest. Hard work needs to be started and finished before the sun is overhead. The same applies if you are in town to see the sites and want the best light in which to view and photograph the monuments and landscape of this unique area.

The real early risers may be up before first light to ride in a hot-air balloon, but the majority who prefer to keep their feet on the ground will in all likelihood be eating breakfast at sunrise on a beautiful cool morning, quite possibly seeing the balloons drifting over the landscape, and experiencing a tingle of anticipation at the day ahead.

If you are inclined to travel independently, it is quite easy to find a driver and plan your own itinerary. Such an approach does entail some extra work, but it will allow you to take things at your own speed and in the order you choose. It also allows you to change your mind and follow fun opportunities that may arise. In Egypt, that's a great bonus.

With many visitors only staying for a few days, local tourism understandably tends to focus on the monuments at the expense of appreciating the wonderful natural environment. In particular, the bird life of this region is abundant and spectacular. If you enjoy the natural environment, one spot to stroll amid greenery is Kings Island (formerly called Crocodile Island). This private island is home to the Jolie Ville Hotel, and there is a great deal to do around this well-planned and established spot. Once there you may wander freely and enjoy the many places to sit under trees, sip coffee, or take a boat ride and feel transported to an ancient ecology. Once again, this is best enjoyed as dawn breaks.

If you are looking for a relaxed retreat away from the cares of daily life, this island offers home comforts and seclusion, with captivating vistas and a gorgeous mix of flowers and trees. The waters and air around the island teem with iconic Egyptian

From your car Egypt can be like a silent movie, forcing you to add your own story to what your eyes observe. It is forever fascinating and often humbling.

birds, such as ibises, hoopoes, bee eaters, and egrets, along with the dramatic pied kingfisher, which performs dynamic dives into the shimmering Nile. Keep an eye out for much rarer birds, such the Nile Valley sunbird. This endangered species resembles a hummingbird, but they are unrelated. If you see a flash of blue, purple, and sunshine yellow, you know you've had a lucky day. Higher up, birds of prey soar gracefully on the thermals. To identify these, binoculars are a must.

When visiting the ancient sites, it is worth remembering the role birds played in Egyptian life and mythology. As visitors move from site to site, such major gods as Horus (the falcon-headed god) and Thoth, who is often shown as an ibis-headed human, appear frequently.

A less peaceful aspect of Luxor life will surely be encountered on the west bank, as vendors thrust tourist trinkets at you while chanting, "Cheap price, cheap price!" At this point,

These painted homes near Madinat Habu invite photography,
and the wish to know more about the rooms beyond

The many layers of Madinat Habu

it is worth remembering a short poem by Lewis Carroll before you are drawn in by even the most charming salesman.

> How doth the little crocodile
> Improve his shining tail,
> And pour the waters of the Nile
> On every golden scale!
> How cheerfully he seems to grin,
> How neatly spreads his claws,
> And welcomes little fishes in,
> With gently smiling jaws!

Often, the first ancient Egyptian monument seen by visitors to Luxor comes as a surprise when they are suddenly confronted by the Colossi of Memnon sitting alongside the road. These huge statues are all that remain of the mortuary temple of Amenhotep III, who reigned in the fourteenth century BC through good times in Egypt. These two enormous seated figures once guarded the gates to Amenhotep's funerary temple, which in its day was the largest in Egypt but has long disappeared under the surrounding fields and the annual Nile floods. Viewed from afar, the two figures seem dignified and complete. It is only up close that one sees the

Light and shadow reveal the stories
on the walls of Egypt's temples

The columns in the first court of
Madinat Habu blend ancient colors
and changing light each day

A modern guardian of the past

The sunburned bases of a once mighty hypostyle hall

ravages of time and nature, but three thousand years have not managed to erase their massive, brooding presence.

Funerary monuments and tombs are an integral part of the experience of Egypt's ancient past. The latter evoke the excitement of exploration and even a frisson of danger as you imagine their creators and decorators, as well as the grave-robbers and discoverers.

Tombs cannot be described as relaxing, being frequently hot, crowded, and (for anyone with a hint of claustrophobia) slightly intimidating. But they are an excellent way to reflect on those who worked in them and the conditions they endured in order to provide a worthy resting place from whence their leaders would travel to the next world. After studying the meticulous scenes depicted on their walls and lit by the changing light, I love to look out at the sky and imagine how it must have felt to finish a day's or a night's work in the tomb and emerge to the fresh air, clear skies, and a sense of freedom. A great deal of the wonder we experience in ancient Egyptian history is based on long, hard hours of dedicated work. Tomb digging and building rank alongside pyramid and temple construction as an extremely arduous task, and working underground must have been particularly unpleasant.

Visits to the Valley of the Kings, as well as the Valley of the Queens and Valley of the Nobles, will reveal astonishing art and craftsmanship. However, the tombs can be cramped. The temples scattered on either bank of the Nile offer many more places to linger, and corners where one can sketch, read, or simply contemplate. Although the major sites have similar architecture and decoration, they vary greatly in feel and scale. The degree to which they have been unearthed, researched, and rebuilt determines how they look today, but all are astonishing examples of early architecture and religious devotion.

The passage of the sun may well determine how long you wish to spend in the temples, and for those who aren't interested in delving deeply into Egyptian history, searching out those dramatic angles of light and shade cast by columns and entablatures and taking pictures is equally enjoyable. (I would mention that if you are with kids, they love deciphering hieroglyphs.)

For those interested in exploring a temple, Madinat Habu is a great site. It is well preserved, imposing yet manageable, and has exquisite paintings and murals in a good state of repair. Built by Ramesses III, this temple from the Twentieth Dynasty follows the style of those built by great pharaohs of earlier dynasties, and has much in common with the nearby Ramesseum.

Much of the peaceful beauty of Madinat Habu is revealed after passing the second pylon (entrance gate), which leads you into the peristyle hall. The massive carved and painted columns create an atmosphere of awe and delight, and repay prolonged contemplation. Every surface, including the ceiling, is adorned with painted carvings that

A traditional home, a New Kingdom temple, and an ancient land

Delicious Egyptian food with a view in the village of Kom Lolah

The fertile fields of Luxor's west bank

draw the eye from one glorious image to another, and then to the countryside glimpsed beyond the next courtyard or column. All the murals tell stories, using archetypal images of ancient Egypt.

Temples fulfilled many functions in ancient Egypt, though their principal role was to commemorate the pharaohs while acting as official places of worship for the gods. Within these complex sites, particular areas were reserved for certain classes of people, and within those, such as the sanctuary space, festivals of differing importance took place. Ordinary Egyptians were not directly involved in the ceremonial life of the temple, but they did come to pray, bring offerings to the gods, and seek wisdom and advice from them.

Sitting in the midst of this relatively intact ancient site, it is easy to imagine how imposing these vast places must have been, visible for miles around. You will find yourself transported back in time, part of the crowd waiting to witness a ceremony celebrating the power of the pharaoh and the priesthood.

As you cast your eye down the lines of columns to the surrounding countryside, it is worth remembering that the building and management of such temples provided a huge boost to the local economy. Erecting such structures

employed thousands of workers, artisans, and priests, and they in turn needed a town to support them. That remains true to this day, as the temples are world-famous heritage sites whose visitors all feed the local economy in the form of shops, restaurants, hotels, and transport.

Take your time and allow the atmosphere of Luxor to sink in. Dwell on what catches the eye so it will remain in your memory. All too often, the sheer scale of what you see in Luxor during a short visit is overwhelming. Seeing everything in a whirl may mean remembering nothing.

As you drive around the west bank, many things catch the eye, not least the local people and their homes in the villages you pass through. Like so many aspects of traditional Egyptian life, people's homes were dependent on the Nile, in this case the soil from its annual flood. Many homes in the west bank of Luxor are still built using traditional methods and materials, combined in some cases with modern comforts added over time.

Mud bricks are the staple material of the traditional house, the mud carried from the riverbank in leather buckets. Once at the construction site, the mud may be mixed with straw and pebbles for added strength before being

One window with three views

poured into molds to dry. The house will be covered in plaster before, in most cases, being painted in bright colors or with scenes of daily life.

Keeping as cool as possible is a must, and thus the windows are kept small but aligned to ensure a good cross-draft from the prevailing breezes. One key design element relating to lifestyle is having the living area on the upper floor and using the roof as a recreational space for eating and socializing, thereby maximizing the fresh, cool air of the morning and evening. Depending on the season, families also sleep under the stars. If it can be afforded, the foundations of such homes are sometimes built of stone, which is longer lasting,

but in all cases the mud home needs constant upkeep to ensure its longevity.

When Hassan Fathy, Egypt's most famous contemporary architect, set out to revive traditional house-building techniques, he told his students: "Build your architecture from what is beneath your feet," and this famous quote has become an article of faith for vernacular architects and builders across the world. A localized building approach is greener, cheaper, and more in tune with the environment. Should you have the misfortune to drive around the ring roads of Egypt's major cities and see the relentless miles of concrete tower blocks, you may regret that Hassan Fathy's sentiments have not prevailed more widely.

For many years known as Chicago House, this traditionally built former research establishment is now a beautiful hotel serving local food and overlooking farms

Across from the entrance to Madinat Habu stands a small café called the Ramses Coffee Shop. The owner's home is a wonderful example of a local house, and also has some of the tastiest traditional food on offer. Furthermore, the restaurant has a stunning view over the temple and surrounding fields. After a hard morning of tourism, the coffeeshop is a relaxing place to sit and watch the world go by, or to try and figure out how many different languages you can hear.

Another welcome refuge in the middle of the day may be found in the courtyard restaurant of the Marsam Hotel. This small but beautifully managed establishment is close to the Ramesseum and is famous within Egyptology circles. It is the oldest hotel situated on the west bank at Luxor, and its

This simple building has hosted Egyptologists, writers, artists, and many others for almost one hundred years

buildings have been used by archaeologists for many years. Missions and institutes from many countries have used this as their base during the digging season. Its simple rooms and spacious courtyard area provide a perfect spot to read, research, and write before relaxing at day's end.

The Marsam was built in the 1920s. For decades it was known as Chicago House, the base for the Oriental School Epigraphic Survey of the University of Chicago, which has been working in Luxor since 1924, before it became a hotel in its own right. Each year, archaeologists from across the globe stay here, and its central areas have served as a place where they, along with artists, craftspeople, scientists, writers, and students, can spend time together and enjoy excellent food and cooling drinks. The view across the fields and nearby excavations is peaceful and calming, while the colorful traditional decor is matched by elegantly simple interior furnishings.

As you look across the lush green land being worked by farmers and animals, reflect on how their millennia of toil have served the varied needs of generations. In ancient Egypt, the majority of the population lived on a principally vegetarian diet, with meat being enjoyed only at festival times or by the wealthy. In New Kingdom Egypt, the staple crops

Traditional food in a colorful, relaxed setting

Filling a balloon with hot air before dawn

included emmer, lettuce, onions, garlic, sesame, corn, chick-peas, papyrus, and flax. Emmer was a vital grain used in the production of two key components of the diet, bread and beer. Barley was also a common crop, as were castor beans, used to produce castor oil.

Until the Romans occupied Egypt in 30 BC, beer was the most popular drink, but with the coming of Rome wine production increased and locals seem to have taken a liking to it. Alongside these pleasure-inducing crops was another—the opium poppy. Thus, some 1,300 years before Christ, Egyptians began cultivating opium thebaicum. Trade in the opium poppy flourished, especially under the reigns of Thutmose IV (r. c. 1401–1391 BC), Akhenaten (r. c. 1352–1335 BC), and Tutankhamun (r. 1332–1323 BC), with opium being exported across the Mediterranean by the Phoeni-cians and the Minoans into markets such as Greece and Carthage. Almost two millennia later, in AD 400, Arab traders introduced opium to China from Thebes. Snippets of history such as this indicate that intrigue must have flourished in ancient Egyptian society, and the Hotel Marsam itself has a compelling family history, which includes tomb robbers and the theft of antiquities from the surrounding hills.

After a good lunch and tea, it may be time to head back across the Nile to Luxor town. These days there is a bridge over the river, but it is some distance away and discreetly hidden from view. A quicker and more fun way to cross the Nile is via one of the ferries that run constantly day and night, carrying all manner of items as well as the busy local folk. For almost nothing—around one Egyptian pound (less than a US quarter) at the time of writing—you can cross the river like a local, have a chat, and enjoy a great view. Scattered along the banks of the river are the shells of boats that have worked this area long and hard, and are left to rot slowly on the riverbank.

The main ferry area in Luxor town is very central, and from there you can choose to head off by taxi, or take the slower but much more enjoyable horse-drawn *kalesh*. Take the bar-gaining negotiations in your stride as part of the experience.

If you're feeling energetic, pay an evening visit to Karnak. If this is your first visit to Karnak you are fortunate indeed, for it's a site that cannot fail to impress even the most jaded traveler. This massive site can absorb immense hordes of visitors, while still providing spaces for individuals to stroll around, read, and learn from its walls and architecture in relative peace.

All year round, many balloons rise over the west bank and drift over the landscape and
monuments of Luxor—a most spectacular Inside Out view

The prime time to visit is very early in the morning, and if you are fortunate enough to be one of the first to enter at close to six a.m., you will have a wonderful chance to take magnificent photographs and wander to the farthest extent of this wondrous site, all the while imagining how it must have been at its height.

Built over thirteen centuries, Karnak was founded around 2055 BC and then expanded by multiple pharaohs. Its central and most awe-inspiring features are the central areas of the temple of Amun, including the Great Court and the Hypostyle Hall.

Karnak is experienced as a series of spaces separated by pylons. These monumental gateways separate out the various courtyards, which draw the visitor farther and farther into this vast site. The pylons are of record-breaking proportions, with the second opening onto the Hypostyle Court measuring 103 meters by 52 meters. The hall itself is perhaps the most extraordinary space in all of Egypt, and is supported by 134 columns, which are 22 meters tall and 3.5 meters in girth.

The temple complex grew from the original Middle Kingdom temple dedicated to Amun, one of the most important gods of ancient Egypt, to a site for the many gods in ancient Egypt's pantheon of deities. The major gods venerated included Hathor, Horus, Osiris, and Ptah. These and any other deities to whom the pharaohs of the New

The temple of Khonsu is a miniature Karnak. You can share its quiet splendor with the resident flock of pigeons.

The face of Tutankhamun as Amun Ra in Karnak, a very fine sculpture

There is no place more magnificent than Karnak's hypostyle hall for understanding the sheer scale of ancient Egypt's riches, power, and devotion to its gods and pharaohs

The ferry crossing the Nile at Luxor is great value and provides
a unique look at local life from inside and out

Kingdom felt they owed a debt of gratitude were honored
with gifts. The priests of these gods became extremely
powerful, and it was they who administered Karnak. Their
roles included the important jobs of collecting tithes and
gifts from those who came to the site. In return, their
community role was to dispense food and give help and
advice where needed. Importantly, it was the job of these
priests to interpret the gods' will for the people. At the same
time, they oversaw a site that at its height covered an area
approximately half the size of Manhattan. So complex was
the organization that, at the end of the Old Kingdom, over
eighty thousand priests were employed at Karnak, and the
high priests were thought to be wealthier than the pharaoh
they protected.

The Aboudi Bookstore has been helping visitors understand the history around them for over one hundred years

A visit to any Luxor temple is an opportunity to allow one's imagination free rein, picturing the buildings roofed in and full of people, and the priests gliding up and down the aisles while going about their duties. No doubt they were places of intrigue and secrets. Do devote at least a morning to Karnak if you can, and then return at night for the sound-and-light show. To know it Inside Out, however, would be a life's work.

The unprepared visitor to Luxor can easily be over-whelmed by the sheer number of sights to see and places to visit. Any attempt to understand pharaonic history, including the gods and mythology of this era, leads to books. Fortunately, Luxor has many places that sell guidebooks and publications on all aspects of Egyptian history and culture.

The famous Aboudi Bookstore has been serving Luxor since 1909 and offers the widest range of books relating to ancient Egypt. It recently opened a restaurant above the bookstore, which overlooks Luxor temple. The latter is in a mixture of styles, and even includes a mosque within its architecture. A view from the bookstore is unrivalled, and what better place to sit and read about ancient Egypt in cool and comfortable surroundings? The Aboudi family have been part of the Egyptian book, photography, and tourism scene for over a hundred years, and their in-depth knowledge is apparent in the range of books sold and their presentation. This is a special place to shop, learn about the past, and relax inside away from the heat of the day.

A taxi ride along the corniche of Luxor provides an encounter
with local life and famous places

PRECEDING PAGES:
The restaurant above the Aboudi Bookstore provides
an unparalleled vista of Luxor temple

Equally enticing, and undoubtedly more famous, is sunset at the Winter Palace Hotel. This is a perfect end to any day out, but as you walk to the hotel along the corniche you may choose to spend a little time in one of Luxor's most famous historic shops, Gaddis and Co., situated in front of the hotel in a lovely location facing the river.

While the decor and design in Gaddis retain all their past charm, the contents are up to date. The shop is beautifully maintained and offers a wide choice of all things Egyptian.

Attiya Gaddis started his photography business in Luxor in 1907. Having begun his career as assistant to the Italian photographer Antonio Beato in the late nineteenth century, Gaddis acquired the Beato Studio in 1907. He went from strength to strength, and became famous as he accompanied many visitors and dignitaries on their trips through Egypt, recording them in thousands of images. Gaddis photographed Egypt from north to south—its villages and towns, ancient sites, landscapes, and peoples. When Tutankhamun's tomb was discovered in 1922, Gaddis became very busy indeed, as thousands flocked to Luxor to follow this thrilling event. As a result, Gaddis decided to diversify, and opened the bazaar, which has been selling all things Egyptian for many years, while housing and selling Gaddis photographs and exhibiting memorabilia such as cameras in their windows. It is a lovely space to shop in, and to gaze out from. The house rules of the owners (still the Gaddis family) forbid hard selling to customers, so you can browse in a relaxed way and make your choices at your own pace. It's a pleasure to spend time perusing the stock, which includes everything from books to jewelry, and from perfume to cotton items. Your shopping complete, carry your treasures up the grand stairs to the Winter Palace Hotel and end your day with a final treat.

The windows of Gaddis and Co. look out onto Luxor's corniche and the Nile beyond

Gaddis and Co. have a fine collection of historic black-and-white photography. The allure of old pictures remains fascinating to each generation of modern travelers.

The bookstore within Gaddis and Co. retains all the fine hallmarks of traditional
bookselling style and provides service to match

The Winter Palace, rather like the Old Cataract in Aswan, combines opulence with rich colonial design and references to the glory of pharaonic times. The hotel was built in collaboration with Thomas Cook by Cairo hoteliers Charles Baehler and George Nungovich. It took two years to complete, and was inaugurated on January 19, 1907, with a picnic held in the Valley of the Kings.

The hotel became the central winter venue for twentieth-century explorers fascinated with ancient Egypt and Egyptian culture. Indeed, it was from the imposing staircase of the hotel that Howard Carter announced his discovery of the immaculately preserved tomb of Tutankhamun, and Tutmania set the world's press alight. The Winter Palace played host to the international press corps and foreign visitors who descended on Luxor to follow the story. Carter used the hotel's noticeboard to deliver occasional news and information on the discovery.

The hotel was also popular with Egyptians, and indeed the Egyptian royal family often stayed in the hotel to enjoy the perfect winter climate and escape the colder air of Cairo. It was here, too, during a winter retreat, that Agatha Christie wrote her famed 1937 novel *Death on the Nile*.

The Winter Palace gardens have hidden corners

In the Winter Palace garden, you may come across the finest example of Egypt's crafts

Looking out to the garden of the hotel, whose shaded pathways and pool provide
relief from the sun after a hot morning of tourism

The historic Winter Palace Hotel in Luxor is a pleasure to wander through.
Each exquisitely decorated room brings the sense of a grand past and high times.

When entering the calm interior of the Winter Palace Hotel, you are following the path of many famous visitors. Sometimes you may be welcomed by the sound of traditional music.

The corridors of the hotel are grandly finished and the scale of space reflects the standards expected by the most luxurious and wealthy Edwardian travelers

The magnificent foyer of the Winter Palace Hotel

Each boat lasts its owner and his family for many years.
They are often painted in bright colors and the boatmen take
pride in their craft's maintenance.

Today it is a hotel that remains aware of its place in history.
On walking in, you immediately feel an air of superior grandeur.
The restaurants, sitting areas, and wide corridors are redolent
of the style and quality of a bygone age. Beyond the lobby you
will find the loveliest gardens in the city, whose trees, grass, and
flowers come as a reminder that the banks of the nearby Nile
consist of the richest soil. Feel free to wander through the lush
royal gardens filled with exotic flowers, as local and migrating
birds visit and feed. Designed to enhance the architecture, the
gardens successfully create open-air "rooms" where you can
linger outdoors under century-old trees.

If, on the other hand, you choose the Corniche el Nil Hotel
to watch the Luxor sunset, you will have a spectacular end to
your day as you contemplate the going down of the sun on a
civilization that revered it thousands of years ago. The sun sets
over the west bank, and the light is scattered as it shimmers
off the Nile. Boats give depth and shape to the scene, and the
occasional cloud will impart a painterly feel to the canvas
unrolled before you.

Feluccas under rare gray skies near Luxor

The last moments before dark reveal pastel colors. No two sunsets are ever the same in Upper Egypt.

The view from the Winter Palace balcony to the Nile and west bank
has been the favorite lookout for travelers over the past century

Sunset on the east bank reveals the many
crafts that ply the Nile at Luxor

Fayoum and the Valley of the Whales—Creativity and Creation

By Lake Qarun are many spots offering entertainment to the families of Fayoum's ever-growing population. A local Ferris wheel provides a new perspective by the waterside.

Water wheels are a rightly famed part of Fayoum history. They have played a major role in the area's agricultural economy for almost 2,500 years, raising water to be transported to the fields, as they still do today.

OPPOSITE: Tunis village has free art to entertain you as you pass through its pretty streets

It is not unusual for urban areas in the world's great cities to rediscover and reinvent themselves generation by generation. This may happen because of rising property values or some shift in the ethnic mix at a certain time. It may be the arrival of a new restaurant or shop, or the growing size of the town itself. In most cases, the effect is positive, leading to better houses and infrastructure. In the case of the village of Tunis, in the oasis of Fayoum southwest of Cairo, it was the lure of potters and their unique style that turned an artisan village into a go-to destination for Cairenes to shop, stay in the boutique hotels, and eat in the restaurants.

The story of the potters is not new, but its impact on Tunis Village's rapid growth is more recent. In the 1980s a Swiss potter, Evelyne Porret, moved to Egypt and established a house and pottery studio. Evelyne was the first potter in the village, and she also trained many of the local children in the craft of pottery. Over time, some of her students established their own studios, and the transformation of Tunis began. Fayoum pottery is now known worldwide. Thirty years after Porret's arrival, artists, painters, writers, and creative people from Cairo and elsewhere have settled in the area and built mud-brick houses in the village. It is like no other place in Egypt and now, with hotels such as Kom al-Dikka, the Sobek Lodge, and

Fayoum, along the edge of Lake Qarun to Tunis village, offers many places to stop and sit, enjoy refreshments, or shop, preferably with some green around to relax the soul

All Fayoum pottery travels the creative journey from the wheel to the kiln, to the store, and eventually to someone's happy hands

Lazib Inn offering lodgings and special organic cuisine, it is possible to turn the two-hour trip from Cairo into a weekend away that is relaxing and, if you choose to take a pottery class, creative and fun.

In addition to the potteries, an art center contributes to Tunis's lively artistic feel and is used by all types of artists working in many different media. It is a communal space, which fuels new ideas and brings together artists of all ages, styles, and backgrounds. Tunis continues to grow, but it already contains a school, over ten pottery studios, and an internationally renowned annual pottery festival.

Tunis is a village island in a green area that, like so many parts of Egypt, continues to be pressured by increasing population and urbanization. Within an area of only a few hundred square meters you can see what Egyptians with creative, business, and social flairs can achieve together.

Fayoum pottery is famed for its constantly changing, individually made pieces. Whatever you buy, you feel you have a unique work every time.

This Fayoum-dwelling cat looks very much at home, because she is

A walk along the pottery-lined main street of Tunis reveals intriguing spots of color
and light to draw customers into the studios

Inspired interior design and local materials make this village home
cool by day yet warm to the eye

These windows on the world of Fayoum life show details of tasteful Egyptian crafts and the building work of local artisans. Beyond the gates and walls lie special places to unwind in a country setting.

The pedestrian street through the center of Tunis village features attractive painted scenes and simple, alluring houses

Fayoum is Egypt's largest oasis, its lakes fed directly from the Nile. Its rich soils have been cultivated since the Middle Kingdom (2100–1750 BC), and it was a particularly successful area during the Ptolemaic period. Fayoum remains a vital agricultural area today, and the land under cultivation is some five percent of the whole of the country. Dotted around Fayoum are many sites of archaeological and natural interest. These are largely under-visited by tourists, but are well worth the effort of making a day trip or spending a weekend away from Cairo.

The geography and habitats of this special area provide ever-changing activities for visitors throughout the year. Bird-watching around the wetlands and ponds is at its best during the winter months as migrating birds follow the Delta and the Nile to warmer climes. The summers can be punishing for outdoor activities, but for hiking or desert sports such as sandboarding, any time from September through April will be fine, provided you prepare well for your adventures. Along the shores of Lake Qarun are numerous local hotels and restaurants to take shelter in and look across the lake to the desert beyond. The waters shimmer in the midday heat and the sands in the distance seem magnified.

North of the lake lies the Petrified Forest of Fayoum in Gabal Qatrani. This is believed to be the largest petrified forest in the world, and features ossified forty-meter-high trees that have survived the glare of Egypt's sun for thousands of years.

The desert area around Fayoum stretches for miles in all directions, and dedicated drivers of four-wheel-drive vehicles can lose themselves within an hour in valleys and plains far from human life. You can be a Bedouin for a day, and find yourself hooked for life on the area's beguiling lands and skies. Standing

Moving from camp to camp on a desert trip gives the traveler views that thrill and a ride that bounces between ever-changing landscapes

The gateway to Wadi al-Hitan marks your arrival at this UNESCO World Heritage Site

In the desert one likes to imagine being far from anywhere and all alone. It is rarely true.

The resthouse at the Valley of the Whales is wonderfully understated, blends in with the landscape, and offers tea or coffee in the welcome shade

out is the sandstone Qatrani Mountain, which is rich in fossils. At 350 meters high, it is a key landmark for Fayum explorers.

As you leave Tunis and the Fayoum lakeside, you turn away from the water and drive toward the Wadi al-Rayan Protected Area and the Valley of the Whales beyond. As you crest a ridge in the road, Wadi al-Rayan appears, taking your breath away. Surrounded by a sea of sand and mountainous rocks, and speckled with vegetation, it is spectacular and inviting. The two lakes that make up this nature protectorate sit in a natural depression well below sea level. Filled with runoff from Fayoum, this large area is home to a diversity of

bird species. Out in the wilder areas are rare animals such as the slender-horned and dorcas gazelles, Rüppell's sand fox, and the fennec fox. Foxes are frequent scavengers around campsites, and their distinctive ears will make them endearing companions during your visit.

The Valley of the Whales (Wadi al-Hitan) is a wonderful treat for anyone with an eye for the earth's ancient past. The area is part of the Western Desert of Egypt, and contains fossil remains of some of the earliest whales, a suborder called Archaeoceti. The recent discovery of these fossils represents one of the major stories in the scientific study of evolution,

The rocky mountains in the desert area around the Valley of the Whales here shine with the late evening sun and an early moonrise

Avoiding the bright sun, even in early morning, is a challenge if you wish to hike in these ancient hills around Wadi al-Rayan

The waters of Wadi al-Rayan have found their way to creating smaller areas of shallow warm waters, which are popular with weekend campers and sports enthusiasts

OPPOSITE: This region has a huge variety of rock formations, many of which lay under the sea millions of years ago

There are several spots to eat and take tea around Wadi al-Rayan's lakes and waterfall.
Here the allure of sandboarding on local dunes has inspired the decoration inside and out.

In Tunis village you can find restaurants offering healthy organic food to
enjoy in a local setting or to take away

Awaking in a desert camp always makes one excited for the day ahead. What lies beyond the dunes and the rocks?

as it shows the transition of the whale from a land-based to an ocean-going mammal. Wadi al-Hitan is the most important known site in the world for the demonstration of this evolutionary stage. A walk through an area close to the visitor center shows the skeletons of whales laid out across the valley floor, and portrays vividly the forms and lives of these whales during this transition period. It is a remarkable visit for all ages, set within a stark and beautiful landscape.

This area also provides a great excuse to spend a night or two under canvas. The visitor center and small shady café area with parking are at the center of a vast area of possibilities. If you hire a jeep complete with drivers, tents, and food, they will do all the work while you eat around the campfire. As you lie looking up at the stars, not far from the fifty-million-year-old remains of sea creatures, you will feel an extraordinary connection to the dawn of the earth.

Cairo—Ever Changing,
Never Changing

Cairo is a megacity with millions of inhabitants, full of noise and traffic. At first glance it may seem impossible to manage in just a few days, but with some judicious planning, the visitor can enjoy many unique experiences. Having lived there for many years, I have highlighted certain areas and walks that I have enjoyed time and time again.

As in Aswan and Luxor, the Nile is central to life in Cairo and one might imagine that, as huge and constant a presence as it is, it would be a simple thing to enjoy day or night. However, it most certainly is not, particularly if you want to sit and ponder the river drifting by while reading or enjoying a moment of quiet. Nevertheless, with some inside knowledge, you can reach the mighty river and savor its special atmosphere at water level.

Visitors and locals alike are in search of that elusive vista, which could be described as a living painting. Bisected by the river's open, natural flow, the city around it takes on a less frenzied sensibility, and the closer you get to the water the farther from the street you feel. To be on the water is to no longer be in Cairo. To be on the water is somehow to feel connected to the magical land of Egypt as a whole.

The Nile is alive all day with craft such as feluccas, racing rowing boats, water taxis, and the occasional police boat or speedboat. That said, in places it is possible to enjoy a few tranquil moments by the vast, empty river, and the sense of serenity and agelessness can be almost overwhelming.

The most evocative of all craft are the houseboats moored along parts of the river, especially on the western bank opposite Zamalek. Here is an entirely separate riverine world that one cannot access without invitation.

Houseboats require a certain rejection of modern comforts in favor of a unique opportunity. To live on the Nile

and wake by it each day justifies any discomfort, but as the photographs show, it is only the view that gives a clue to the houseboats' location. Indeed, the interiors of the boats I have visited reflect the owners' tastes and origins.

Given that so many of the houseboats are occupied by people from Western cultures, it can feel as though one is leaving Egypt to sit by the Thames, the Hudson, or the Seine—a nice little break. However, to sit outside on the terrace at water level for breakfast or at sunset is to know you are in Egypt.

Kitkat is the neighborhood to head toward; it took its name from that of a former houseboat that served as a notorious drinking den and drew lovers of a seedy nightlife in the early part of the twentieth century. Today the boats seem more sedate, but who knows what goes on behind the gates and walls of trees that protect them? Those I visited were certainly more sedate than saucy, though, despite the seductive alternative lifestyle they offer.

The small procession of wooden houseboats opposite the northern end of Zamalek is the residue of a once-thriving community from a period when they ran the whole length of Cairo. Not only were they home to residents, nightclubs, and casinos; they also harbored wartime espionage in the form of the German spy Johannes Eppler, whose arrest was portrayed in the novel *The Key to Rebecca*. At the center of the scandal was Hekmat Fahmy, the most famous dancer at the Kit Kat Cabaret. She was said to have seduced British officers and extracted information from them, which she passed to Germans who used a houseboat as their base.

Not far upriver are various rowing clubs, whose riverine locations around Zamalek and Giza provide great places to get close to the Nile and see another aspect of the city. Rowing in Egypt is, at its more serious end, dominated by clubs attached to the police, armed forces, and universities.

A quiet houseboat near Kitkat Square

The Nile at dawn, from inside one rowing club looking out onto another

Nevertheless, it is possible to take to the water in a scull at the more public clubs, such as the Egyptian Rowing Club.

All through the year, Egyptians young and old work out by the Nile and run along its corniches, and many get to row. The view of the city from such places, and from the boats, is a treat for the senses. Early risers can encounter a whole world of activity, fun, and breathtaking sunrises to set you up for the day ahead, or for a glorious weekend, in the knowledge that you have done something unusual, healthy, and rather special.

In the process, you will become a part of a long, although not continuous, history of the sport, which was a feature of ancient Egypt, when galley rowing formed part of regattas held in Luxor. After the pharaonic period, it seems to have fallen into obscurity as a recorded sporting pastime, although the Nile was no doubt just as busy with boats as it is today. During the Second World War, when the British troops stationed in Cairo started building racing boats, interest in the sport was rekindled and, over the next quarter of a century, many boathouses arrived on the banks with their accompanying clubs. In addition

Summertime means an early start to beat the heat

to the well-known rowing teams from the police, major companies such as Arab Contractors also founded rowing clubs, followed later by the Cairo University Rowing Club and others.

In the early 1970s, Egypt reemerged internationally in the sport, when the Arab Contractors Club participated in the Henley Regatta in England, as well as competing in the United States. Soon after, the annual Nile Rowing Festival was launched. Now that Egypt is firmly back on the world rowing stage, the sight of men and women of all ages and backgrounds indulging in a healthy pastime against an amazing

backdrop is inspiring. Five Egyptians (three men and two women) qualified for the London Olympics in 2012, indicating the levels achieved in the modern era and the interest and encouragement shown to both sexes.

Anyone can go out on the Nile for a small charge and experience one of the oldest forms of sailing in the world. Some things in life become a cliché and lose their sense of being special, but sometimes, as with the felucca ride, a cliché is such a thing because it is true. Taking a felucca is a must, and one of the best Inside Out experiences one can enjoy in all of Egypt.

The Sofitel lobby is a fine spot to plan your next outdoor venture

In Karl Baedeker's 1908 *Guide to Egypt and the Sudan*, he recommends hiring such boats, which are used for the transportation of sugarcane, cotton, and other goods, and adds: "No luxury of course, must be looked for, but its absence is compensated by the close relations with the land and people, into which the traveler is brought." He also notes that "a young attendant with some knowledge of cooking may be obtained for £E 2 to 3 per month [less than one dollar these days] who will also do the necessary marketing in the villages." It is easy to imagine the felucca captains of today being part of a family line that steered such travelers and goods in times long gone.

With the sunset, the light changing from gold to orange, and the sense of quiet accompanied by a light breeze, a felucca trip at day's end will soothe the soul of any traveler.

Zamalek's northern tip has one of the most idyllic spots in Cairo from which to look Inside Out—Sequoia restaurant

Let go and absorb the atmosphere of the Nile and the gentle swirl of the water.

Now we return to the southern tip of Gezira Island and one of the most spectacular hotel settings. The Sofitel, formerly the Sheraton El Gezirah, is a circular hotel with views in all directions. Looking at this opulence today, it may come as a surprise to learn that this island only emerged and separated fully from mud banks in the nineteenth century. It was in fact only stabilized as a place to inhabit after the opening of the first Aswan Dam. The southern half of the island (the northern end being Zamalek) was later laid out by the British, who had been granted access by Khedive Tawfiq.

This hotel is in as central a place in Cairo as you can get. Lying in the middle of the river, in the heart of the city, and at water level, its unsurpassed view is a sight to behold when you need to get away, or to really celebrate. An hour or more spent gazing out from within the hotel or its gardens will both recharge your batteries and remind you of the space Cairo fills. Looking around at the combination of buildings, sky, and water truly gives a sense of the vastness of the space around you.

Across the water from the houseboats, at the northern tip of Zamalek, is a complex of restaurants open from early morning until deep into the night, with Sequoia at the center of this delightful corner. With views north to the Imbaba Bridge, and with the east and west banks of the Nile far enough away to allow one to appreciate the quiet calm of the river at one of its widest points within the city, this is an island within an island.

Sitting here, it's surprising to reflect that less than one hundred years ago, this was a spot reached by ferry from the Bulaq area to the east, then the city's river harbor and a key transport hub linking the economy of the Delta with markets in Upper Egypt and Cairo. Zamalek's art deco blossoming was just beginning, as the northern end of Gezira Island was bought for development and divided into plots for resale in 1905–1907.

As you can see from the photographs, the setting of this restaurant is truly delightful at sunset, and is a place to enjoy a unique sense of people and place, as the well-heeled local clientele make this a lively spot late into the night. For much of the day, however, or during midweek, it can also be a haven for those who seek some quiet to read or think. The river

The grounds of the Cairo Opera House provide a welcome shaded walk

The El Sawy Culture Wheel is an oasis looking out onto the cramped towers of Zamalek beyond

traffic of working and pleasure craft is a reminder that one is in the midst of a busy place; Cairo is a megacity.

The place to really get close to the river is the El Sawy Culture Wheel, situated beneath the busiest bridge crossing the island and spread across an area that was once a garbage tip and no-go area. Muhammad El Sawy opened the cultural center in 2003 and dedicated it to his father, Abdel Moneim El Sawy, author of a string of novels with the series title *The Wheel*.

Now an established part of Cairo's cultural life and a real oasis for people of all ages, the Culture Wheel plays a major role in encouraging artistic expression and provides a venue for both new and established artists and musicians.

The overall feeling of being in what is almost another city altogether allows escape from the hubbub just beyond the gates. The light at day's end and at night can be magical. For an even greater sense of escape, you can take the water taxi from under the bridge.

The Culture Wheel is both an indoor and an outdoor experience, but the greatest secrets of Cairo's architectural past lie inside the residential buildings of Zamalek.

I obviously cannot encourage the reader to wander into other people's homes and buildings uninvited, which is a pity because, as anyone who has ever strolled around Zamalek knows, it is the most tempting of places for those who love interior style and design.

The beguiling glimpses into the foyers of the buildings on either side of 26th July Street are part of the mostly expat syndrome I call "see beyond the *bawwab* (doorman)." All buildings have a guardian of some kind, although in the new century the quality of security and general standards of cleanliness seem to have fallen away. In times past, being the front man for a building was a role to be admired and a job done with pride.

There are many buildings that have some business role to play, such as hotels, restaurants, bars, cafés, and bookstores, which means you can legitimately enter them and wander around.

Life beyond the doorman in Zamalek is exciting

Zamalek has reinvented itself in some buildings with elegant stores and bric-a-brac emporia. Great for browsing.

Zamalek's Sufi Bookstore and Café is a haven for students, away from the babble of the world outside

The glass door of Diwan Bookstore is a window familiar to all Zamalek book lovers

This tiny selection of pictures gives some indication of how Zamalek at ground level is repurposed. Here we have hotels and art galleries, stores and bookstore cafés, and the neighborhood is nirvana for those with a staircase or elevator fetish.

There is an architectural tradition of building tower-like structures in major cities across the globe. Usually commissioned by men wishing to make a mark on both the present and posterity, they dominate the skylines of their cities. The Cairo Tower is Egypt's version of this phenomenon and is, by world standards, one of the more attractively designed and eye-catching examples of its kind. Like the Pyramids and other members of the tall-building club, size matters, and the scale of this tower is impressive.

Built in 1961 and inaugurated by Gamal Abdel Nasser, with a recent and successful refurbishment that has added changing light effects at night, the Cairo Tower is well worth a visit. At 187 meters tall it is a long elevator ride to the top . . . or some 2,500 steps, if you wish to stretch your legs. At the top are restaurants and the viewing gallery. As with many of Cairo's more elevated landmarks there is a certain element of luck to this, but the view on a clear day will take your breath away. To see across Cairo to the Pyramids and the Citadel, and to see the Nile winding far to the north, explains the geography of the city better than any map.

With plenty of variety and modern grandeur, Downtown Cairo manages to retain a personality separate from the rest of the city. This sense of age and prestige stems from its unique mix of architectural styles and the area's distinctive position as a crossing point for all the major events of Egypt's recent history.

These days it requires no small feat of the imagination to see the center of Cairo as it was when Khedive Ismail's nineteenth-century dream of a "Paris by the Nile" became a reality.

Les Livres de France are famous Cairene booksellers. This was their store on Brazil Street in Zamalek, looking out on the green road beyond.

He had returned to Cairo after a visit to the 1867 Exposition Universelle in Paris, where Egypt's pavilion had been a huge success in presenting ancient Egypt and the Orient as the next exciting travel destination. The khedive, however, was more interested in bringing Europe to Egypt, and set about developing a downtown district that imitated the quarters of Paris in style and design.

Today there remain enough major streets and statues to evoke a European-style city, although daily life has clearly imparted a distinctly Egyptian flavor to Downtown.

However, there are lots of interesting interiors to explore, which can be done over the course of a one- or two-day slow wander through the places chosen here—if you pace your journey and look beyond the crowds and noisy traffic.

A good place to begin is one of the easiest to find. The American University in Cairo (AUC) these days runs most of its classes on its vast campus in New Cairo, but its well-preserved original building sits proudly on the edge of Tahrir Square and has witnessed many of Egypt's most volatile and moving events of the last hundred years.

The American University in Cairo's beautifully decorated Oriental Hall and staircase

Once you are on campus, you can choose to sit either inside or out, for it has some of the prettiest gardens for miles around and offers a shady place to relax, read, and plan one's walk. It is also a good starting point if you wish to visit the AUC Bookstore, which offers a wide range of books on Egypt in English and other languages with which to accompany your visit.

The buildings comprising the original campus include some attractive neo-Islamic architecture, which has been lovingly maintained. The main building facing Tahrir Square, the Khairy Pasha Palace, has an elegant foyer and staircase, which offers a cool interior lit by stained glass and with exquisite geometric designs. It was built in the 1860s by the then Egyptian minister of education, Khairy Pasha, as part of the early development of the new Downtown Cairo district.

One room that will take your breath away is the recently restored Oriental Hall, situated by the fountain courtyard at AUC. While not open to the public all the time, it is usually accessible during working hours. Every inch of this small space is decorated to the highest standards.

Setting out for Downtown thankfully takes you away from Tahrir along the nearby Talaat Harb Street. Here a quick visit to the Oum El Dounia gift shop and bookstore allows for a more elevated view of the area from their terrace. From that vantage point, one's imagination may travel back in time as far as one's historical knowledge permits, but for me it is hard to be in such a spot and not recall the days of Egypt's 2011 revolution.

Nearby, in Bab al-Luq, is another high spot that exemplifies the Inside Out experience and remains a cherished haunt for many foreign visitors. The Horreya Bar has many facets, which create a sense of either enjoyment or expectation, along with some occasional low-level anxiety. Having been a visitor on many occasions for some thirty years, my enjoyment of this unique space and atmosphere depends entirely on the context of my visit.

On those occasions when the nearby streets are simply too loud or crowded, Horreya offers a sanctuary (though not a cool one on hot days, as there is no air-conditioning). A cold drink and a shoeshine make a winning combination, giving you a chance to watch the world go by and speculate

The mirrors of the Horreya Bar afford great opportunities for discreet people-watching

on the lives of the others sharing your moment of escapism. Horreya is a split universe, with floor-level windows for the no-alcohol end and, these days, a darker end with the light cut out for those enjoying Egypt's finest beers. The light that moves through the room over the day picks out every detail in this spot, which, despite a recent renovation, has already reverted to its one-star shabbiness. The glimpses of the surrounding street and its conservative people, reflected in the Stella Beer mirrors, highlight the contradictory attitudes to drinking in Egypt. The best to time to visit is late evening, when the bar is at its cosmopolitan best. The interaction of foreign visitors and Egyptians makes for a noisy mix and has done much over the years to encourage friendships and understanding. Opinions are not sought; they are expected. Once inside the Horreya, it is unlikely you will get out that quickly.

The bar of the Windsor Hotel transports you to another time and place while you enjoy the quality of its light

Leaving the Windsor's front door plunges you straight back into the city's animated street life

The Windsor elevator shaft casts light through the center of the whole building

The graphic style of the Café Riche is seen here Inside Out and back to front

If you're seeking a more sedate late-afternoon experience to wind down the day, you could do no better than visit one of the world's greatest time capsules on Alfi Bey Street just off 26th July Street downtown—the renowned Windsor Hotel.

In truth, few people see more of this classic hotel than the public areas of foyer and bar, but despite this its atmosphere is strong enough to leave a mark in the memories of all visitors.

In fact, the Windsor was not purpose-built as a hotel. It was originally a bathhouse for the Egyptian royal family at the end of the nineteenth century before serving as a British officers' club for many years. Eventually it was purchased by a Swiss hotelier as an annex to the famous (now destroyed) Shepheard's Hotel in the nearby Azbakiya Gardens, and operated as the Hotel Windsor–Maison Suisse.

The period feel one enjoys today in the famous barrel bar and breakfast room are as close as you can get to being in authentic colonial Cairo, and the possibility that you might find yourself sharing a meal or drink with the family owners is a refreshing change from corporate hotel management.

Sobhy Greiss (left), born in 1901, opened the Anglo-Egyptian Bookstore in 1928; his son, Amir Greiss (right), then ran the store after him. Amir's sons are now in charge.

A wrought-iron staircase uses minimum space, as books are king in the Anglo-Egyptian Bookshop

The key to the Windsor is its silence. Find a seat by the window and allow yourself to read or ruminate while enjoying a private view of the streets outside. Depending on which side of the room you are on, the view is a coffeehouse, a junction, or a street of food vendors, all busy with people who don't look up. From your secluded perch, you can sit and simply observe life, a soothing way to pass the time of day and ponder the glorious, ever-changing light.

For a less refined experience, visit the Café Riche on Talaat Harb Street, one of the most iconic spots in Downtown Cairo. Whether your interests incline toward politics, art, literature, or modern history, this café has something to offer. Its atmosphere is unique and the view onto the street from the quiet calm of a historic interior provides a window onto modern Egypt, where epoch-making events took place.

The seemingly unchanging decor, staff, and food and beverage offerings create an experience to be savored. The walls are adorned with photographs and artworks depicting Egypt's most famous writers, musicians, and artists, including Nobel laureate Naguib Mahfouz.

A landmark of Downtown Cairo since it opened in 1908, numerous stories of intrigue surround the Café Riche. The

1952 plot by Gamal Abdel Nasser and the Free Officers was hatched in and initiated from the Riche. Sixty years later, during the 2011 revolution, the café was an ideal distance from everything that was happening in Tahrir Square and managed, perhaps because of its respected place in Cairene history, to survive even when fighting and chaos swirled around it.

Felfela restaurant, off
Talaat Harb Street,
hosts an eclectic range of
decorative objects

The light through Felfela's roof makes for a colorful lunch

In addition to food and drink, Downtown offers another cultural treat, one that is rapidly disappearing elsewhere in the world—the old-fashioned bookshop.

Wandering around the streets of Downtown it is still possible to understand why the khedive wanted this area to emulate Paris and commissioned French architects to bring that sophisticated European feel to nineteenth-century Cairo. His dream was the rapid development of Egypt, and to achieve that he chose to follow what he saw as the best in the world at that time. No surprise then that, with such beautiful buildings and rich denizens, many bookstores opened in the area. A number remain, but few offer the wide range of European languages once available. When I first arrived in Cairo to sell books myself, I was impressed by the quality of the bookstores, but the decline in quality stores owned by genuinely expert booksellers is one of the reasons Downtown is losing its cultural appeal to the European traveler.

Nevertheless, a stroll to Muhammad Farid Street can include several old bookstores, including the famed Lehnert & Landrock and Reader's Corner, both on Abdel Khaliq Tharwat Street; the latter now offers framing services.

The Anglo-Egyptian Bookshop has been a great center of academic and educational bookselling for three generations. Here is a place to browse for unexpected delights. The Greiss family tradition of building a stock of books and showing patience in selling them is refreshing in the fast-moving retail world of the twenty-first century. The high ceilings and tall bookshelves are accompanied by well-informed assistance from loyal and intelligent bookstore staff. The cool interior is just a window away from the hectic road, and this lookout (especially if you are offered tea or coffee) is a great little stop on your journey around Cairo's modern heart.

Eating is a significant part of daily life in Egypt, and countless restaurants and fast-food venues line Cairo's myriad streets and alleyways. Some are beloved by Egyptians and some are well known to visitors. Outside of hotels, however, there are few places where Egyptian cuisine can be genuinely enjoyed by both. Felfela has been one such place since 1959.

The restaurant's somewhat crazy interior design is a true delight. Careful examination of walls and ceilings show it to be a half-open-air restaurant that could only survive in a hot, dry country. The food and service are great value, both for the quality of meals and the opportunity to sit and watch a restaurant at work. All around you is evidence of famous past visitors and of busier tourist times.

The harsh daylight is suffused into cool, almost church-like colors, which create a soothing atmosphere, but Felfela can be enjoyed at any time of day or evening. The food from their grill is excellent, and some dishes, such as shakshuka and Dawood Pasha, are not readily found elsewhere.

After this, a short walk to Talaat Harb Square and Groppi may provide a fitting finish to your day or a sweet start to your evening.

This busy circle in the center of multiple streets hosts a statue of Talaat Harb, a leading Egyptian economist and key figure in his country's economic and financial life in the early part of the twentieth century. He stands surrounded by a ring of recently renovated buildings that boast a heterogeneous mix of architectural styles, which is part of what makes Downtown so special. When viewed from Groppi, the famous confectioner's store, it is indeed a grand sight.

Groppi was a global brand till the end of the 1950s, and their chocolate creations were world-renowned. Their tearoom was *the* place to be seen, and foreign royalty frequently paid a visit. Now it is none of these things, but the place retains an unmistakable charm.

Beyond the mausoleum of Sultan al-Ghuri
lies the path to Bab Zuwayla

The play of light as you move around is delightful

Bab Zuwayla's twin minarets are a steep winding climb,
which one often shares with other visitors

City Gates to the Muqattam Hills

Part of the allure of Cairo is the ability to travel back in time while wandering through the city.

One such journey starts by the Khan al-Khalili bazaar and takes us south and east to the City of the Dead and the Citadel before we arrive above Cairo at the Muqattam Hills. Medieval Cairo is an intensely cramped area of narrow streets and historic buildings that fill the space between the modern highways of al-Geish and Salah Salem streets, an intense visual and aural experience for any visitor.

In fiction, time travel involves an instantaneous transition from one place and time to another—to the future, the past, or perhaps a parallel universe. In medieval Cairo, this change occurs as you pass between the magnificent buildings that comprise the Sultan al-Ghuri Complex, with the mosque–madrasa on one side, and the mausoleum and *sabil-kuttab* (a public water facility and Qur'anic school) on the other.

These two edifices stand guard at one entrance to Mu'izz li-Din Illah Street and the crushingly busy path toward Bab Zuwayla, Fatimid Cairo's southern gate, and one of just three remaining of the city's many historic entry points.

The short walk to the actual gate of Bab Zuwayla is absorbing and sets the tone for the places you may choose to visit in the area. The juxtaposition of the man claiming to be Cairo's only remaining fez maker and the store opposite, selling gaudy new underwear and lurid belly-dancing outfits, provides one of those moments when you are caught between past and present.

There are innumerable buildings and places to see or stop at in this complex area, and the examples given only scratch the surface. Soon the tall, powerful minarets of Bab Zuwayla loom before you and you arrive at what feels like a gateway to history.

This gate, built in 1092, is important architecturally as an example of work by the Fatimids, who brought with them the techniques of stone masonry for building the new city walls and gates. The Fatimids invaded Egypt from Tunisia and founded what we now call Cairo (al-Qahira—the Victorious) in AD 969. Over the next two hundred years they introduced a North African influence in mosque design, before their overthrow by the great warrior Saladin and the beginning of the Ayyubid Dynasty.

From these twin towers you have one of the great Inside Outs of Cairo. The steep climb inside them is the precursor to a wonderful moment when you emerge at the top and look around in all directions over the oldest part of Cairo and the evidence of its long history.

Bab Zuwayla is a popular spot with Egyptians and visitors alike, and a good place to take pictures. The panoramic view provides an excellent opportunity for orientation. Below the gate is the mosque of al-Mu'ayyad, which forms part of the same complex and was completed around 1420.

On your descent back to street level, allow yourself to drift back in time, although not all the thoughts may be romantic oriental visions. True, this gate was the starting point for the caravans to Mecca and the south, but it was also the site for executions. In the sixteenth century it must have been a place to visit with one eye on an escape route, as it was associated with all manner of street life and the false hopes offered by miracle healers.

At ground level you pass through the gates itself and are assailed by sights and sounds from all directions, although by now your thoughts may be turning to a glass of tea in a cooler place. The near end of Shari' al-Khayamiya, or the Street of the Tentmakers, beckons ahead.

The Street of the Tentmakers was built in 1650 and is the only covered market street left in medieval Cairo. Its aim then was to provide the tents, cloths, and saddles for those setting out on the pilgrimage to Mecca in the great caravans of the day. It has remained largely unchanged, and indeed is populated by families who in some cases can trace their heritage of appliqué-making back over almost four centuries.

The enormous mosque of al-Mu'ayyad stands next to Bab Zuwayla

Refreshingly cooler than Mu'izz Street, and illuminated with diffused sunlight, the Street of the Tentmakers is a welcome break from the surrounding streets. While its expert craftspeople continue to make goods to order, their mainstay is the output of appliqué quilts and bags destined for the tourist market.

If you have been given a rough time by hawkers in the Khan al-Khalili or at the Pyramids, the soft sell with tea or lemon juice here is a delight. If you relax and go with it, a highly enjoyable conversation may ensue. Furthermore, you will find out that everyone here really does know the craft they have been trained in.

The mosque of Ibn Tulun would top many lists of the greatest buildings in Cairo. It is certainly my favorite, and indeed I would argue that, with its simple elegance and geometry, Ibn Tulun is one of the world's great architectural secrets. Long may it stay that way, so it can be enjoyed for its relative quiet and sense of peaceful strength.

Ibn Tulun is also the ideal spot for a wide variety of Inside Out experiences. Its layers of courtyards and doorways, arches and crenellations, and unique (in Egypt) minaret all provide delightful places from which to look out on the passing world. When work began in 876 on this massive Friday mosque, no one could have foreseen that, just over a thousand years later, this space would be surrounded on all sides by high-rise

The Street of the Tentmakers remains a working and trading center which
makes visiting and observing most exciting

Between the inner and outer walls of Ibn Tulun is a wide area of extra defense and architectual variety (above). On each side the play of light and shadow reveals more of Ibn Tulun Mosque (left).

apartment blocks with roof dwellers and satellite dishes as far as the eye can see. The roads around the mosque are an area of extreme human density, and the sudden sense of quiet and emptiness when you enter the mosque is disarming.

Ahmad Ibn Tulun was sent to Egypt from Baghdad in 868. By the time he began building this great mosque, he had risen from being governor of Fustat to being the first ruler of an independent Egypt since Cleopatra. By refusing to pay tribute to the Abbasid caliph he effectively proclaimed himself the founder of a new dynasty.

The mosque of Ibn Tulun will deliver a wonderful experience, something hard to guarantee for most excursions. It can also provide some of the most evocative photographic opportunities in Cairo. Unlike many mosques, it is rarely busy, and one is able to wander freely almost everywhere. When I wax lyrical about Ibn Tulun to Egyptian friends, I am often surprised to find they have never been. Then I remind myself that there are many places in London I have never been to either. It's easy to forget the most remarkable things on your doorstep or put them off for another day.

Al-Azhar Park has been a huge success in terms of providing a green public space for Cairo denizens while bringing fresh beauty to Islamic Cairo

If, after so much wandering through busy and cramped streets, you seek some refreshment and fresher air, nearby al-Azhar Park is a good choice.

Al-Azhar Park is a miracle of modern Cairo. It lies just outside the eastern limit of medieval Cairo, squeezed alongside the busy motorway that is Salah Salem Street. Despite these cramped surroundings and the need to remove five hundred years' worth of garbage from a huge area, the project, funded by the Aga Khan Foundation for Culture to the tune of some US$30 million, created an oasis covering thirty hectares. The

park provides much-needed green space for Cairenes and has been celebrated ever since it opened in 2005.

The restaurants, pavilions, gardens, walkways, and quiet seating areas in the park provide wonderful views across Islamic Cairo and the city in all directions. The Moorish style of the buildings and courtyard are something out of an *Arabian Nights* fantasy, especially if you gaze toward the Citadel, which is about a kilometer and a half away. Many things come to mind as you stand and absorb the vista, but for me the message is one of hope. Al-Azhar Park is proof that

The Inside Out perspective from al-Azhar Park's
restaurant area displays the gardens' geometric design

Taking a photograph from the Citadel wall is a must-do for your Cairo trip

with determination, cooperation, and vision anything can be turned around.

Throughout this trip around Cairo's historic heart, one feature will have been a constant in the corner of your eye. The Citadel that sits high above Cairo is the former impenetrable fortress of Saladin, who founded this garrison town after his arrival in 1168.

Cairo, and indeed the whole of Egypt, was ruled from here for the next seven centuries under various rulers. It was only some 170 years ago, however, that the mosque of Muhammad Ali, which has become one of Cairo's most iconic symbols, was built. The mosque of Muhammad Ali is, for many, the Citadel proper. Its imitation Ottoman style represents a key moment in the return of Egypt as a regional leader during that period of Turkish dominance.

Standing at the wall and looking west across the whole of modern Cairo as far as the Pyramids of Giza is a sight to which no photograph can do justice. It is a massive panorama. From inside the mosque itself, or from the courtyards and seating areas, every view is spectacular. The city below, especially the older and Islamic areas, still have a sense of age that transports you.

The famous labyrinthine market area of Khan al-Khalili, which is the shopping destination for all tourists and many Egyptians, abuts the great market street of Muski; together they comprise an area where you will find anything but the truth. Perhaps the only thing on which everyone seems to agree is that the Khan al-Khalili is named after Jaharkas al-Khalili, an emir of the Mamluk period, who was active around 1382. It was also known as the Turkish Bazaar.

The Citadel is one of the most visited and photographed places in all of Cairo

The view over the rooftops of this old part of the city includes al-Azhar Mosque

Avoid the middle of the day and wander the back streets when the slanted light brings magic to the Khan al-Khalili

This is a place to be single-minded if you wish to find and buy a desired item at a price you like. Equally, it can be a place to wander, take photographs, and enjoy a coffee or honey-filled *fitir* (sweet flaky pastry) at the inaccurately named Egyptian Pancakes restaurant. However, the thickness of your skin will be tested by the constant harassment of salespeople and you must take the experience with a smile.

It's easy to imagine the centuries of stories that underpin the place we see today. Families who have traded here for years and have seen everything are effectively battle-hardened. They bargain with equal measures of charm and steel. If you are prepared to wander boldly, it is an ideal space to enjoy different views and find unusual perspectives. The main streets are strewn with tourist items of variable quality and even more variable prices, but venture farther inside and high-quality gems can be found. Remember that, with shopping as with many other things, beauty is entirely in the eye of the beholder, and nowhere more so than in the Khan.

Fishawi Café is that rare example of a tourist trap that does not disappoint

Mu'izz Street's buildings are still and quiet while outside the constant flow of hooting traffic navigates these narrow old roads

As you wander the buildings of Mu'izz Street, consider the wonderful decorative aspects of these great spaces

OPPOSITE: The Hammam of Sultan Inal is an elegantly kept memory of the glory days of bathing in the Khan al-Khalili

My only tip when you're tempted to buy is to hold whatever has taken your fancy for thirty seconds and examine it properly. This allows time to consider your choice and tends to scare the salesperson into reducing the price without your actually having to speak.

If you look above ground level, there are hotels for leisure and local business visitors on a budget. They overlook a large square and the mosque of Sayidna al-Hussein. This is a highly venerated place and one of the few mosques that do not encourage non-Muslim visitors. Friday prayers take place in the square outside, and these can be observed without entering the mosque.

No visit to this area is complete without taking tea or coffee while the world of commerce comes to you. Fishawi Café is a special place to do that, lying as it does close to Hussein Square, the Khan al-Khalili, and Midaq Alley (famously featured in the novel of the same name by Naguib Mahfouz). The role of Fishawi and its success is based on catering for tourists and locals alike, as well as appealing to all ages. Given that the café claims to have been open twenty-four hours a

From the Hussein Hotel breakfast room you can view al-Azhar Mosque, which every Friday draws thousands of worshipers

day for the past two hundred years, it must be succeeding in this balancing act!

Adjacent to the Khan al-Khalili is the impressively renovated Mu'izz li-Din Illah Street, where, in just a few hundred meters, you can visit almost every building and be transported to the exotic East of the *Arabian Nights*. The interiors offer a sense of otherworldliness that fits the Hollywood portrayal of the magical Orient.

These majestic interiors all look out at some point onto modern-day Cairo through the windows and *mashrabiya* (carved wooden latticework) screens. In some cases, the light floods from above onto courtyards, or streams in through colored glass. I find this quiet, assured sense of historic space, so close to the real world just feet away, a marvelous crossing point from the imagined past to the less attractive reality that engulfs you as you head home.

You may have seen the flags of the Fontana as you drive along the Sixth of October Bridge. Next time make a visit.

The Fontana's bar is simple but functional

Old Cairo to Maadi

It seems almost unfair for one city to have such a depth of historical treasures within its walls, but Cairo has been blessed with concentrated areas of astounding historical importance.

Thus, within a few minutes' stroll of each other are several of the earliest and most beautiful churches, as well as Egypt's oldest synagogue.

The Hanging Church, the Church of Saint George, the Church of Saints Sergius and Bacchus, and the Church of Saint Barbara are all focal points in the history of the Coptic Church and, while they have all undergone renovation over the centuries, the sense of being in a truly old place of real importance is palpable.

What is termed Old Cairo is defined by the ancient city walls known as Babylon, which served as a Roman fortress in the third century AD and is believed to have been the place where the Holy Family found sanctuary during their flight to Egypt. There are many sites associated with this visit scattered along the Nile. The family is said to have passed through

The narrow, winding streets of Old Cairo have a natural sense of being both indoors and outside

Qantara, the Delta, and Heliopolis before finding safety from Herod's reach in what is now an important area in Christian heritage and history.

At the time of their arrival, this tight, narrow-walled community was something of a forgotten enclave, as it was in Alexandria that culture and art thrived under Greek influence. The large Jewish community that lived in Babylon is still celebrated here, as evidenced by the beautiful, recently renovated synagogue of Ben Ezra, which is surrounded by the churches of early Coptic Egypt.

The biblical stories that underpin the history of Old Cairo are mirrored in the vast array of paintings and artifacts that fill every corner of the churches and play a key part in the daily devotional life of the very active Coptic population, which now numbers over ten million across Egypt.

These historically rich streets have seen Jewish, Christian, and Muslim communities who lived side by side in shared spaces

Leaving the Hanging Church and its ancient history, you are struck by the encroachment of new buildings

Windows in the Church of Saint George

The foyer of the Manial Palace draws on Turkish and Moorish influences

crazy mix of interior styles that shout opulence at every turn. As you wander from room to room, it is easy to imagine the conversations, social whirl, intrigue, and glamour of the incidents that occurred within the walls of the palace itself and carried great influence beyond them.

The prince was the uncle of King Farouk as well as his chief regent, and the son of Khedive Tawfiq I. As such, for much of his life he was the heir presumptive of Egypt and Sudan, until the birth of King Farouk's son, Ahmad Fouad. Soon after this, Egypt was declared a republic and, like many members of the royal family, the prince left for exile in Europe. He died in Lausanne in 1955.

The royal heritage in Manial Palace and its grounds has created one of the few places where one can feel close to that period in Egypt's history. The popularity of King Farouk has ebbed and flowed in Egypt but fascination with the man and his time has endured, as evidenced by the wide range of visitors to the palace.

From an Inside Out perspective, these buildings and grounds have it all. Period styles of the highest quality combine with architectural brilliance to keep the rooms cool, light, and functional. The textiles, carpets, and furniture that fill the rooms are also of great beauty and interest.

After luxuriating amid the greenery and being able to wander at will, you may wish for more of the same. Heading south to Maadi is a good option. Just a few stops on the metro line bring you to Road 9 and its many shops and restaurants.

Maadi is a relatively modern part of Cairo, known for its wide roads, large villas, and green spaces. The area was developed into this modern suburb at the start of the twentieth century, originally planned by a Canadian named Alexander J. Adams immediately after the opening of the railway line from Cairo to Helwan. It grew in size and importance during the Second World War as a base for the large number of soldiers from New Zealand, who chose the area as a rather luxurious home for themselves.

Just a short journey away, on Roda Island, is one of Cairo's greatest yet least-visited treasures: Manial Palace. If you wish to experience royal history and get a feel for the Ottoman-era glories of late-nineteenth-century Cairo, a long, leisurely visit to Manial Palace and Museum is a treat for the eyes and soul. The huge walled area contains several buildings connected by pathways through a fine collection of trees and plants, which provide quiet corners to sit and rest between the various highlights of your walk around the complex. Any time of day is a delight.

The palace was built by Prince Muhammad Ali Tawfiq in the early part of the twentieth century, and is a somewhat

The house as a whole includes inspiration
from Morocco to Persia

The mosque in Manial Palace is
a masterpiece of Islamic style, and one of
the most ornate spaces in the complex

Flower shops bring color and life to many street corners in Maadi

Road 9 in Maadi has many cool and quiet stores to explore

Looking out onto Road 9 you will find people shopping and eating 24 hours a day

Traditional stores such as ironmongers are owned by proprietors who have spent their whole life in the business

In the small mini-markets off the main road are other specialist stores and interesting denizens

Newer businessmen take advantage of Maadi's younger, family-oriented customer base

When heading to any of the Cairo pyramid sites, do detour to the Ramses Wissa Wassef Art Center to see their world-famous weavings, beautifully displayed here

In modern times, it is hard to believe that Maadi had noise-after-dark regulations, as well as rules ensuring all gardens were kept in good order. Although there are still many beautiful gardens, they are often hidden behind walls and trees.

No one can say they have been to Cairo without making a trip to the Great Pyramid of Giza, but, as with many trips to iconic monuments, a visit can be somewhat underwhelming. Decades of construction and hordes of visitors have virtually destroyed the atmosphere around the site, but with a bit of planning, you can add on some side trips that will make this day out truly memorable.

As you head toward the southern edge of Cairo and finally sense you're leaving the city behind, the concept of Inside Out changes. The main difference is the never-ending sky once the city's tall buildings and heaving streets are left behind. Do make a short detour, however, and visit Dr. Ragab's

Pharaonic Village for a look into ancient Egypt's creative past. This often-ignored tourist trap is as close as you can get to Luxor without actually going there and is lots of fun for locals and foreigners alike.

Rather bizarrely, the best full-frontal view of the Pyramids and the Sphinx is through the upper windows and roof of the Pizza Hut opposite the main entrance to the Giza site. This jarring juxtaposition of past and present is highly entertaining, and if you go there after visiting the site itself, it will feel relatively peaceful and much more relaxing. This is a view that really cannot be replicated anywhere else in the world.

Another place to escape the hustle and bustle is the bookstore that faces the Pyramids and Sphinx. After experiencing the Pyramids up close, you may wish to read more about them, or buy pictures that reflect your visit. The store is cool, and the light filtering through the doors encourages browsing and sitting in the chairs provided.

The Pyramids are physically tough to engage with—after all, they were designed for the dead rather than the living. While it is possible to go inside the Pyramids at Giza, you would be lucky to have them to yourself, and in all likelihood you will be one of many inside a suffocating space. This experience is certainly not for those suffering from claustrophobia. By far the best overview of the Giza site is from the desert. This can mean a camel ride, and I would urge you to do that, even if it seems a typically touristy thing to do. Negotiate hard, and then relax once you are aboard. The image of the Pyramids so close to the vastness of Cairo beyond will stay in your mind forever.

Some thirty minutes away are two of the best archaeological sites in Egypt. Both provide the chance to escape and appreciate the landscape and special nature of Egypt's fertile land.

Saqqara and Dahshur, the two largest sites after Giza, include pyramids and tombs to explore, but also allow one to appreciate how the culture of the Old Kingdom grew around these extraordinary first forms of stone architecture in the Third Dynasty (Old Kingdom), during the reign of Djoser

Leaving from the inside to the light beyond always comes as a (literal) breath of fresh air

Looking out from the parking area to the Bent Pyramid is exciting for visitors as they arrive

(2667–2648 BC). During his time, Egypt enjoyed a period of peace and stability. Supporting Djoser was one of Egypt's most influential figures—a man named Imhotep, whose vision created the Step Pyramid.

Just south of Saqqara are the Bent Pyramid and the Red Pyramid. These ancient sites would dominate most countries' tourism industries due to their sheer size and historical interest, but in Egypt they are just a little too far from the city for the majority of short-stay visitors.

One of the main reasons Dahshur and its delights are so sparsely enjoyed is that the recent history of this site included years when it fell inside a military area and was closed to public access. Over those years, an out-of-sight, out-of-mind sensibility prevailed and the pyramids were largely forgotten by tourists. This situation, combined with their relative distance from the city, created the semi-isolation that can be enjoyed now.

The so-called Bent Pyramid is a marvel of survival. How did it get built and how has it remained standing? With much of its casing still intact, it is at once well preserved and incomplete.

Standing above the edge of the desert by the fertile farmland of the Nile Valley, it is a testament to bad mathematics. This is probably a harsh judgment, however, on what is thought to be the pharaohs' first attempt at a true pyramid, built around 2600 BC on the orders of Sneferu, the father of Khufu, who built the Great Pyramid at Giza.

The Bent Pyramid is incomplete in that it was never used for its intended purpose. When it became clear that the angle of building was impossible to maintain from the base to the summit, the pyramid was topped out at a lower angle. Its abandonment (a sense of which prevails even today) is to my mind the very essence of its charm. Visit in the cooler times of year and you may have the site all to yourself. Picnic there

Many ages run together in parallel when you are near the Pyramids

Depending on your budget, Pizza Hut (above) or the Mena House Hotel (opposite) offer very different experiences but both deliver amazing views

and walk around at ease. There is a smaller, collapsed, pyramid nearby that one may climb if it is quiet. It is also a terrific place to take photographs.

The so-called Red Pyramid, which can claim to be the first successfully completed true pyramid, can today be visited and entered.

Looking up the ramp that takes you from below ground to the exit high above is a unique experience. Picture the workers or the pharaoh's senior figures doing just this some

five thousand years ago. You can imagine their sense of relief when they emerged and looked across an Egypt empty of today's cities and roads, and perhaps in annual flood.

I have saved a special place with which to end our Inside Out visit to Cairo. The pure enjoyment felt when looking out from the Mena House Hotel at any time is unique in world travel. This famous place has true Grand Hotel heritage, having started life as a hunting lodge built by Khedive Ismail before being used as a rest house for the empress Eugenie.

After she opened the Suez Canal and left, it became a hotel that has since hosted a multitude of famous politicians and celebrities. The views from the restaurant or bar in the original building are breathtaking, and represent the perfect version of Cairo Inside Out. Every era is in view, from ancient Egypt to the modern day, with colonial grandeur all around.

The sense of time travel and glamour are delicious and the interior is a veritable museum. The pool area and gardens also provide a welcome quiet place to escape the tourist hassle just beyond the hotel's gate. Egypt has much to offer and in some places retains its history with style and aplomb. The Mena House has all this and more, and is well worth the journey.

FOLLOWING PAGES: Few bars in the world can compete with this Inside-Out panorama at the Mena House

Alexandria and al-Alamein— Coastline of History and Literature

Alexandria and its Mediterranean coastline are alluring destinations for anyone wishing to escape the heat of Cairo or drawn by the romantic associations of its two-thousand-year history and its place in the literature of Shakespeare, E.M. Forster, Lawrence Durrell, and Naguib Mahfouz. Finding that idealized past is no easy feat, however. I advocate a parallel approach—namely, being aware of the city's past but also appreciating its more modern side, absorbing the remnants of ancient civilizations and exploring modern architectural gems. Then perhaps you will experience, as Lawrence Durrell did, "the one city which for me always hovered between illusion and reality, between the substance and the poetic images which its very name aroused in me . . . Alexandria, the capital of memory!"

A meal by the harbor is an essential starting point to allow you to settle into the very different weather and seaside vibe that Alexandria enjoys. The thrill of an infinite horizon and the presence of a sea breeze come as a delight if you have been in Cairo for too long.

Like so much of Egypt, the population pressure in this city of just over five million is all too obvious in the traffic and when walking about downtown, but the expanse of the main harbor provides an escape that always seems close at hand.

From your café you can survey the vibrant corniche and the boats moored in the harbor, while reading up on the city and its long, important past. Many coming here will want to visit the sites of epic Second World War battles and the accompanying cemeteries, but first let us linger awhile in Alex.

Alexandria, with its maritime setting, classical history, and more European sensibility, is a perfect place to escape to for a weekend or more. Go there and you will be inspired.

Overcrowding is a problem but there is always a way to provide a space for people to sit and chat, looking out to the harbor, even in the very center of the city

This set of flags is intended to attract every possible Egyptian to stop at this beach for tea or coffee

Riding an Alex tram often brings you parallel with several other forms of transport, including feet.
The busy-bee colors of the city taxis always raise the spirits after the rather bland white of their Cairo counterparts.

The buildings that stretch for miles along the seafront suffer the damage of sun, wind, rain, and salt but maintain a stoic grandeur that still speaks of a historic past

Perhaps you will dip into one of the novels written about the city and begin to understand its allure.

For many years, Alexandria was the capital of Egypt, and today it is the country's second city. It is full of noise and bustle, with yellow-and-black taxis buzzing along the corniche that forms the barrier between Egypt and the Mediterranean Sea.

However, despite being a second city, Alexandria need not live under the shadow of Cairo. Constantly expanding, with a history as rich as that of Rome, it will never be left behind.

Getting to know Alex is not easy if you wish to claim it as a second city for yourself, but it is more than possible, in a weekend, to explore and find your own few special spots. You'll begin to observe a very different type of local life from either Cairo or Upper Egypt. From then on, regular short visits will peel back the layers of history and you will discover many more places to relax over coffee and cake, while you read, think, or simply look off into the middle distance pretending to be a writer.

The Spitfire Bar is an Alexandrian treasure, a suitable place to enjoy an 'Ice Cold in Alex' beer. I suggest you look it up if that means nothing to you, and then watch the movie.

A whistle-stop weekend that leads to a lifelong love affair has been the case for many since the start of the twentieth century. Those falling for the charms of this city came mostly from Europe. Greeks, French, and Italians have all left their mark on the architecture, food, and artistic heritage that have made Alex rich and famous.

The wooden trays here await a fresh catch of fish. Each owner has a distinctive mark on his own stack.

As you wander the back streets and squares today, conjuring the former glories may sometimes require quite a feat of the imagination, but after the often suffocating atmosphere of Cairo it is always a pleasure to be in this city by the sea.

For it is the sea that gives Alex its special allure. Even when the sea is out of view, the light of the Alex sky allows you to discern where the buildings end and the sky and water begin. It's a lovely feeling that infuses you with a sense of freshness as you walk or drive around. Nowhere else in Egypt has this. As André Aciman wrote in his memoir *Out of Egypt*, describing the expulsion of his family and other Jews from Egypt during the Nasser epoch: "Your senses immediately warn you that if you thread your way through the narrowest of streets, you'll eventually be led to this dazzling expanse of turquoise and aquamarine."

While Cairo may often boast of a new hot spot, which opens with a bang only to close with a whimper a few weeks later, Alex has more places that have aged well. For sure, the younger audience for coffee and *shisha* has created various trendy spots, but some of these, such as Teatro, offer events and performances in keeping with their proximity to the Roman amphitheater, giving a quirky, artsy side to the city.

The restaurants and stores that line the seafront all provide a room with a view

Spend a weekend exploring modern venues or relaxing in the comfort of old favorites.

One historic haven has been part of the city for almost a hundred years. Calithea, a bar and restaurant facing the sea by Midan Saad Zaghloul, was started by two Greeks, Michel Mikas and Constantine Papasis. It is a typical taverna, serving classic Greek dishes and many local favorites to the steady stream of visitors who drop by to sit and chat while enjoying the sea view alongside their food and cigarettes. The smartly suited gentleman who serves you has that special knack of

making you feel like his first-ever customer, even though he may well be a good deal older than you. Farther inside is the bar, which is presumably more lively at night, and has a slightly seedy and careworn air that suggests years of use by thousands of customers. During the day, however, it is a good place to sit and watch the ever-changing light across the harbor.

As you look out across this formerly cosmopolitan, seafaring city, you would do well to remember that Alexandria has been through many waves of both triumph and decline since it was founded in 332 BC by Alexander the Great. It became

A walk along the corniche at any time of day provides artistic inspiration from the city and its maritime history

one of the Hellenistic civilization's greatest cities, as well as the capital city of Egypt under the Ptolemies (ending with the death of Cleopatra in 30 BC) and Romans (when the country was a province of the Roman Empire). At that time it was the largest city in the world, and also home to the largest Jewish community in the world.

Its two harbors have been the gateway for incoming visitors and the exit from Egypt for many traded goods, not least the vast exports of Egyptian cotton that brought such riches to Egypt in the late nineteenth and early twentieth centuries.

The buildings erected during the resurgence of Alexandria as a wealthy trading city during that period are the cornerstones of downtown Alexandria's heritage, proclaiming a sense of past grandeur as they stand, impassive, in the midst of today's much less cosmopolitan city.

The influx of foreigners to the city inspired more than buildings, however, and these days much of Alexandria's appeal for the independent traveler involves soaking up the atmosphere of its literary representations, whether in the poems of Constantine Cavafy; *Alexandria: A History and a Guide*

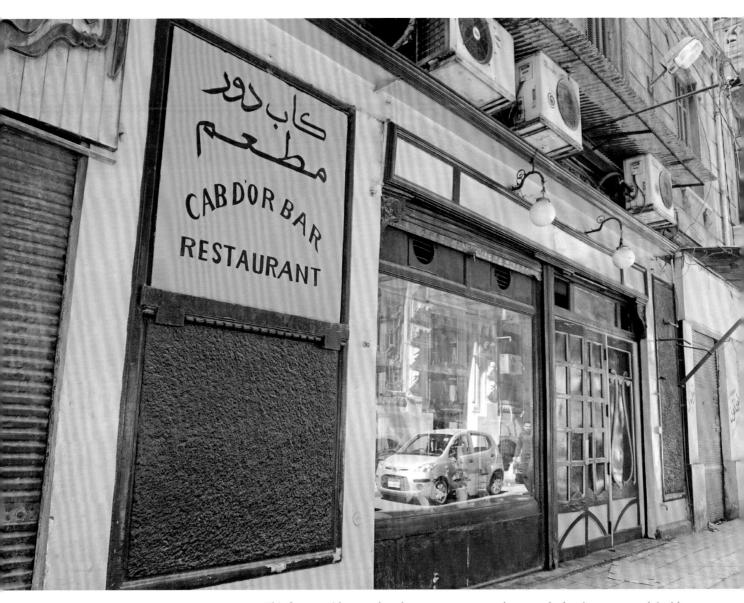

This famous sidestreet bar does not encourage photography but is cozy enough inside;
its windows do not allow you to look out

The eastern harbor, looking out

by E.M. Forster, written during the First World War; or the works of Lawrence Durrell, who lived and worked in Cairo and Alexandria during the Second World War as a press attaché. The Alexandria-born Cavafy was a Greek writer who drew on Alexandria's entire past in his poetry. Keen aficionados of his work can visit the small museum in the apartment where he lived a few streets from the Opera House, which has recently been renovated. Later, the cosmopolitan nature of the foreign artistic and diplomatic community in Alexandria was depicted by Durrell in his most famous work, the four novels that comprise The Alexandria Quartet (1957–60). Sadly, the house where he lived and wrote was demolished in 2017. A very different portrayal of the more modern city is given in Naguib Mahfouz's great work Miramar (1967), which is set in postcolonial Alexandria. This short novel allows Mahfouz to offer an Egyptian perspective on the role of Alex at the very center of Egyptian history and society. Miramar is a perfect read for the visitor with an afternoon to spare in a quiet spot with a view.

The corniche and main square, ringed with hotels, coffeeshops, bars, and restaurants, lie at the heart of the

The Bibliotheca Alexandrina is visible from all over the harbor. When the challenge to build it was set, the notion was of a structure that created a sense of the sun rising from the sea. Here we see that the challenge was more than met, and the building is now a truly iconic success.

FOLLOWING PAGES: Out beyond the harbor you can finally meet the sea, where the Mediterranean reaches Egypt's shores and local people hope to catch a fresh meal

Which place provides the finest view of Alexandria? This is a much-debated question, but looking back toward the city from the Greek Club is high on any list, with its fine food and service as a bonus.

Alex experience. There is no better place from which to orient oneself than the great Bibliotheca Alexandrina, designed by the Norwegian firm Snøhetta. This modern architectural gem was inaugurated in 2002, the culmination of a long-standing dream to replicate the great Library of Alexandria of antiquity, which at its height was one of the key libraries and centers of knowledge in the ancient world. The new library is an architectural marvel. With space for eight million books, it also contains galleries for temporary exhibitions, permanent exhibitions, and a planetarium. Its position facing the sea gives you the chance to get a sense of Alexandria's unique harbor setting, while the thirty-two-meter-high main reading room with its coffered glass ceiling provides a compelling Inside Out experience. It also has a large bookshop, which is the best place for cultural books and gifts in the city.

On the other side of the crescent-shaped bay stands the Qaitbay Fort. The fort was built by Sultan al-Ashraf Sayf

The foyer of the Metropole Hotel is an ideal spot to wait for friends or to prepare for a day out. Whichever way you look out, there is much to see in the busy street outside.

The Metropole Hotel sits in the center of this seaside city,
its rooms providing a faded elegance befitting Alexandria's famous literary past

al-Din Qaytbay in the fifteenth century, and in its time was one of the most important forts in the Mediterranean. It was constructed on the exact spot where the Lighthouse of Alexandria once stood. The lighthouse, one of the seven wonders of the ancient world, was destroyed in a four-teenth-century earthquake.

If you wish to go further back in time, visit the Roman catacombs of Kom al-Shoqafa, which were discovered in the early twentieth century, not far from the Roman structure known as Pompey's Pillar. Recently, excavations have also uncovered the Roman amphitheater of Kom al-Dikka.

However, you may be in Alexandria for a break from antiquity. If that's the case, one of the most enjoyable walks is from the library along the corniche to the Greek Club, which sits at the end of the harbor wall. Distances can be deceptive in this curved space. The club may look a few minutes away, but it can easily take an hour or more, especially if you stop off along the way. It is well worth the effort, though, and the Metropole Hotel, the Cecil, or the Windsor Palace all offer great chances to rest with pastries or pastis and a view of either the sea or the bustling street. At the lower end of the budget, but with higher levels of street experience, the corniche cafés offer all types of Egyptian food and drink, plus the ubiquitous *shisha* bars. The atmosphere is one of slow enjoyment and observation. If your walk is getting too tiring, take a horse and carriage for the last part, or, should it be in the morning, pay a visit to the fish market. This fascinating building is filled with the morning's catch and the range of fish and sea creatures on offer is certainly wider than your average corner fishmonger. Alexandria is famous for its fish restaurants. The Greek Club is the best of all, and has the added bonus of Greek side dishes and a fantastic view looking back toward the city. However, there are others well worth a visit, and rather less expensive.

The Zephyrion is a longer journey in the other direc-tion, but worth the trip if you combine it with a visit to the Montazah Palace and gardens in the east of Alexandria. The Zephyrion, which was founded in 1929, has a superb location close to the beach. Its name means "sea breeze"—something you will need during an Alexandrian summer lunch.

The Montazah Palace is in fact a complex of palaces built by Khedive Abbas II in 1892, during Alexandria's heyday. It remained in royal hands until the revolution of 1952 and today is a large leisure complex with gardens, beaches, a hotel, and a museum of the Muhammad Ali era.

FOLLOWING PAGES: The skyline and bay of the eastern harbor of Alexandria provide the classic panorama seen in photography and cinema for many years. Its long waterfront leading to the sea can provide enough entertainment and fresh air for any visitor.

Whether you seek wonderful seafood or more usual Egyptian fare, Alexandria has some of the finest family restaurants in the country

By the harbor is Alexandria's fish market, a place to visit early when it is full of the fresh catch of the day and the hubbub of traditional commerce

For a wonderful mix of Egyptian salads and fresh seafood, visit Kadoura, on a side street near the harbor, and sample whatever they have on offer that day. Surrounded by other happy eaters, you'll have a real sense of leisurely Mediterranean dining.

Above all, Alexandria invites the visitor to wander. Take a tram ride, and visit a museum or one of the many historical sites that allow you to understand more of the vast history of this city. It is a place that touches all senses. The feeling of being able to take time out and observe life going by makes this seaside city an ideal break from Cairo. The more time you give it, the more you will know it Inside Out. Like so many places in Egypt, the opportunity to step back from the hubbub of street life allows you to understand the place you are in, and also allows you to know yourself.

The Roman Amphitheatre in Alexandria is at Kom al-Dikka and well worth spending time at.
It is the only surviving such monument in Egypt and is sited among pleasant gardens and other
archaeological remains of the period.

OPPOSITE: Alexandria's Shatby area is filled with cemeteries reflecting
the city's cosmopolitan past. There are beautifully maintained
memorials as well as forgotten, unkept graveyards. Here we see, top
and bottom left, the crosses of many Armenians, and bottom right a
headstone in a small French cemetery.

Al-Alamein

The sheer size of Alexandria and its spread along the north coast have created a linear urban area, which is enveloping places that formerly stood alone. Al-Alamein and its war cemeteries have become part of that urban sprawl.

The two battles of al-Alamein took place in the summer and autumn of 1942, with the second battle in October–November marking the culmination of the North African campaign between Allied forces commanded by Field Marshal Bernard Montgomery and the Axis forces (German and Italian) led by Erwin Rommel. For both sides, the objective

was the control of the Mediterranean, the Suez Canal, Middle East oil supplies, and the supply route to Russia through Persia. The Allied victory, the first in the Second World War, came at huge human cost on all sides, and historians have debated whether this victory changed the tide of war, and why the Germans had decided to advance into Egypt in the first place.

When I visited these heartbreaking sites in 1988, they stood alone between the desert and the sea, with no buildings or resorts in view. It was possible to imagine how distant the soldiers must have felt from their homes and families. As testaments to the bravery of all those who died, these

With its panoramic window view of the sea, the Italian War Memorial is a space in which to look out on the past and the present, and wonder what lies beyond the horizon

The Italian Memorial is naturally lit and cool, with a star-shaped skylight that allows the desert sun to diffuse light across the interior to great effect

The Italian Memorial has walls covered with the names of the dead. Its simplicity of design and color, combined with the 4,800 names surrounding you, stop you from thinking of anything but the madness of war.

carefully maintained monuments are magnificent in their silence. There are three large sites to visit, all close together and open to anyone.

As you drive along the coast road today, you will see the Italian War Memorial between your car and the sea, and perhaps you will spot a rock by the road with the inscription "Mancò la fortuna, non il valore" ("We were short on luck, not bravery"). The sentiment applies to all the soldiers buried here. The site of this mausoleum has a spectacular view and its interior allows you to look out to sea and consider the madness of conflict while surrounded by the names of 4,800 Italians and the further 38,000 who are still missing. The white marble structure contains a chapel, and a mosque and a small museum stand nearby.

Al-Alamein's German Cemetery sits between the road and the sea. Built in the shape of a fortress, it contains over 4,200 burials from the Second World War, and 30 more from the First World War. Like all these memorials to the brave soldiers of battles in the desert, it is beautifully tended.

The stairs that takes you to a roof of this memorial echo with the reverential silence that pervades all the monuments in this area

The German Memorial is regularly visited, and moving personal tributes and photographs are left by families.

Should the site appear closed, simply wait a few minutes and the gatekeeper will arrive. Visitors are sporadic and the keeper makes sure the building is spotlessly kept when no one is around. It is worth chatting with those who work at these sites, as they are very knowledgeable.

Around seven kilometers west of al-Alamein is what at first appears to be a large sandstone fortress overlooking the sea. This is the German War Memorial, a beautifully made and well-kept monument to some 4,200 German servicemen. Inside this silent space is a courtyard with a central obelisk decorated with flowers and touching notes from visitors and the families of those who died in this battle, a key moment in the North Africa campaign in 1942. Again, the keeper is most helpful and will, if asked, take you onto the roof for a breath-taking look out to both sea and desert—a chance to ponder the pain and bravery of all those who fought here.

On the other side of the road, facing the desert, are signs to the al-Alamein Commonwealth Memorial. The open-air aspect of this huge site and its individual graves will provide a greater sense of the atmosphere in which the soldiers lived and died on the battlefield where the fighting surged back and forth between 1940 and 1942. The front line was a thousand kilometers of desert between Alexandria in Egypt and Benghazi in Libya, and in this cemetery lie many of the fallen, brought back from the front and eventually buried under stones that simply state "Known unto God."

The El Alamein War Cemetery is an immaculately kept, quiet, and moving tribute to the land and air forces of the British Commonwealth who lost their lives here and across North Africa and the Near East during the Second World War. Soldiers buried here are mainly those who died during the Second Battle of El Alamein in October 1942 and the fights that preceded it. There are over 7,000 graves, of which 815 are unidentified.

FOLLOWING PAGES: The empty, rough beach of al-Alamein provides a quiet spot to ponder the lives that were lost around this area

Marsa Matruh and Siwa Oasis— Sapphire Waters and White Desert

As you travel west along the coastal road from al-Alamein to Marsa Matruh, the roadside buildings begin to thin out and more glimpses of a beautiful sea appear to your right, with desert on your left. Marsa Matruh itself is a holiday town known for its huge, shallow lagoons and white beaches. Set on a large bay, the resort stretches along the shore. West of the town is Cleopatra's Beach, surrounded by rocks that create a natural pool called Cleopatra's Bath.

If you continue to the tip of Marsa Matruh's eastern peninsula you will find a quiet, rocky shore, which is lovely for swimming. Near the beach is the cave system where General Erwin Rommel, often referred to as the Desert Fox, established his command center to wage military operations during the Second World War. The caves are now home to a small museum. All of this is surrounded by extraordinarily blue sea and salt-white beaches.

Marsa Matruh, like so many other cities in Egypt, has expanded tremendously in the twenty-first century. It started as a small fishing town during the ancient Egyptian period and remained thus during the time of Alexander the Great (356–323 BC), when it was called Amunia. Ramesses II (1279–1213 BC) built temples in every part of present-day Egypt, including Amunia. In 1942, the famous Egyptian Egyptologist Labib Habachi discovered the ruins of the temple dedicated to Ramesses by the beach near Umm al-Rakham.

There is a wide variety of hotels along these stretches of blue sea and sands, one of the most iconic being the Beau Site Hotel. It was opened in 1959 by Dimitri (Mitso) Madpak and his family, and has become known as a gem of the

Looking out on the Mediterranean from Marsa Matruh reveals the bluest seas around all of Egypt

Mediterranean. It is one of the few high-class hotels in Egypt that are still family owned and operated.

Over the years, the Beau Site has grown from a small and simple hotel to a perfectly kept family resort, whose rooms have views to transport you from the real world for a while. However, that feeling of quiet isolation dissipates when you head into the hot and busy town. In July and August, Marsa Matruh heaves with Egyptian holidaymakers, and the sidewalk cafés fill with men smoking *shisha* pipes and women shopping. They also come to eat in the easygoing seafood restaurants that line the streets, serving locally caught fish and calamari grilled over hot coals and served with fresh salads, flat bread, and baba ghanoush.

On our journey we stopped at the Beau Site for a morning drink and sandwich, and were transfixed by the vivid view;

Almost as far to the west as anyone gets, Marsa Matruh has spectacular bays, white sands, and perfect seas

Most of the hotels in Siwa offer plain home comfort and a lovely welcome

some five hours after leaving hot, dusty Cairo, it was like entering an azure dream sequence.

Feeling refreshed, you will be ready to contemplate the long ride south through the desert to Siwa, the oasis close to Libya, which lies 320 kilometers directly south of Sallum, the Egyptian frontier port on the Mediterranean coast around 650 kilometers west of Cairo and the Nile.

Siwa is the northernmost of a string of oases that stretch from Egypt across the Libyan desert in depressions where, due to the higher natural water table, springs emerge. In ancient times, these oases were known to the local people and Bedouin travelers as the "Islands of the Blessed." Sighting one of these havens must been a relief to those who had trekked across hundreds of miles of sand. These days, a good road and speedy vehicles have made the journey easy. However, drawing close to Siwa after a long morning's drive still elicits a powerful emotion.

Siwa consists of several oases in a large depression measuring around fifty kilometers long and ten kilometers wide. It sits around twenty meters below sea level and is surrounded

Siwa has a lovely climate, and a lazy time between the palms is the way to chill out

Warm from the oven, Egyptian bread is a meal in itself

by much higher limestone and sand landscapes, creating a sense of drama to rival the most romantic visions of the desert seen in the movies.

Siwa is one of the least known yet most interesting places in Egypt. Though it is now more accessible than ever, it is still far from anywhere and this remoteness is key to its special nature and unique society.

Its small population of desert people are not Arabs, but rather the descendants of Berbers. Berbers were nomadic and existed mostly across North Africa between Tunisia and Morocco. They claim to have been the original dwellers of the Western Desert. Even now, they speak a language of their own, Siwi (which is only spoken, not written), and have managed to maintain their culture since the seventh-century Arab invasion.

The sense of a people different from the rest of Egypt is quickly apparent. Siwa is a conservative place with its own culture and family codes, which means interaction with local

Sitting in a local café allows you to watch all modes of transport pass by on a working day

people beyond the tourist guides and shops is minimal. Tourism is important to the local economy, but Siwa has not sold its soul to feed that beast. Wandering through the town, one feels more like the observed than the observer. So much of the now globalized world lacks such a clear distinction, as the endless stream of tourist traffic through famous sites ultimately overcomes many places' sense of self. Siwa has no such problems.

The ancient Egyptian name for the oasis was "Sekht-am," meaning "palm land." The oasis was then the seat of the oracle temple of Amun (Zeus Ammon), and the site was already famous when Herodotus visited. The oracle was famously consulted by Alexander the Great, a fact that draws many history lovers to visit Siwa each year.

After many wars and attempts to subdue it by various leaders, Siwa only became officially part of Egypt when Muhammad Ali (1769–1849) finally began his conquest of the Egyptian oases in 1819, a costly but ultimately victorious series of expeditions.

Siwa encompasses a large area, and is a launchpad for deserts that would otherwise be inaccessible. The Siwan experience for today's visitor can be divided into three.

First is the town itself, called Shali by the local people. The name is often erroneously believed to be the name of the ruined fortress, which sits at its center by the marketplace. The site is meant to be protected and is already in severe disrepair, but tourists are able to wander around its fascinating paths. A visit at sunset to take pictures is a must. One can

Siwan culture has always been more conservative than most of Egypt, and many of its traditional ways continue today

easily imagine this ancient town as the location for a movie. Around Shali are hotels, shops, and restaurants, which are most appealing in late afternoon and early evening. Siwa is not a party town. The Albabenshal Lodge, built into the ruins, has a superb rooftop restaurant that is beautifully lit at night and serves great local food. Eating there becomes a communal experience, as everyone has traveled so far to get to Siwa that they are eager to share their excitement.

If you are working outward from the town, your second experience will be tours of the oasis itself, and whatever romantic ideas of distant, water-filled islands of fruits and palms you may have, Siwa certainly delivers.

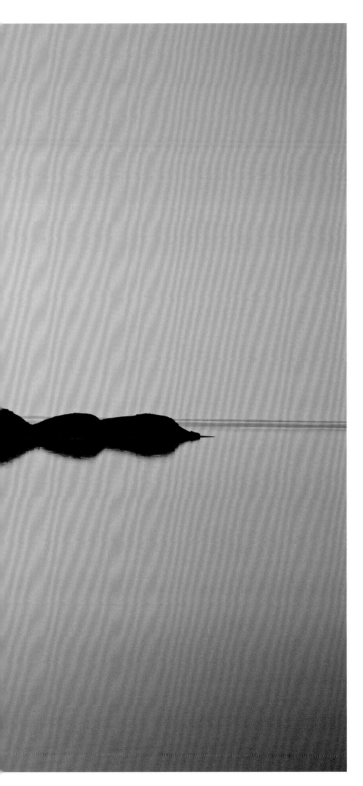

Siwan salt is some of the world's finest and is exported
across the planet from these beautiful lakes

Early morning by a Siwan lake is about as
perfect a view as one could ever enjoy

The carefully chosen objects and design of these retreats are part of what makes Siwa
seem away-from-it-all, but not so far as to make you anxious

Hidden from the usual busy streets you can find
small gems like this home-turned-getaway spot
among the palm trees

This welcoming spot is surrounded by the oasis and sits by a salty spring to swim in

Within the oasis, which stretches for miles, can be found small restaurants, and places to swim and drink coffee, that make a day out in the heat manageable. Make sure you stop by the Temple of the Oracle in Aghurmi, where you can look out in all directions from the summit of the temple and imagine Alexander the Great consulting the oracle following his victory in liberating Egypt from the Persians in 331 BC.

The other spectacular hill with a history is Gabal al-Mawta, a large natural rock formation filled with tombs of both the Twenty-sixth Dynasty and the Ptolemaic period.

While interesting to wander around, they don't reveal much information.

The third experience—and, for many, the greatest thrill in Siwa—is going on a desert drive or, even better, sleeping in a camp overnight while being looked after by a Bedouin driver. There are several small oases that fulfill all one's expectations of isolation, legend, and visual beauty. The driver will light a fire and brew tea while you sit under trees or swim in the crystal-clear warm springs. Looking out from an oasis to the desert sands and skies is an inspirational Inside Out experience.

Siwa knows how to embrace travelers
who have come from afar, and need to
have time to sit back and relax

The Temple of the Oracle is an intriguing warren that was the heart of the settlement of Aghurmi from 663 BC

If your group is alone, you will have an amazing sense of freedom and separation as you look up at the stars, enjoying the silence (or being as loud as you like). If you are with other groups in an overnight camp, you will make new friends as you meet over a simple fireside meal.

Siwa is renowned for its salt lagoons, which produce fine salt for export. The journey to the lagoons passes lakes, trees, and birdlife, culminating in a vision of glistening white natural salt set off by the blue sky and golden sand.

Salt blocks were used to build the Adrere Amellal Ecolodge, some fifteen kilometers north of Shali, which delivers the ultimate extravagant stay. Built entirely from local resources, including beds made of local salt, the lodge has no electricity but provides a unique hotel experience for the very wealthy. If you are looking for a truly mind-expanding sunset, head to palm-covered Fatnas Island.

From any high point the expanse of this vast oasis is breathtaking

The incredible salt hotel called Adrere Amellal has forty handbuilt rooms and blends naturally into the landscape. No part of the hotel has electricity; your stay is lit by the sky above and by beeswax candles.

The rooftop restaurant of the Albabenshal Lodge sits, quite literally, in the heart of the Shali Fortress of Old Siwa. Its unique setting, surrounded by a fascinating ancient city, creates a special dining experience.

The Bedouin drivers of Siwa have four-wheel-drive vehicles to take you on a thrilling but often bumpy desert trip. The landscape of steep, soft-white sand dunes, jagged rocks, and oases is unlike anywhere else in Egypt.

A delicious cup of local tea is made all the sweeter by your surroundings and the service of your driver

The Red Sea and Sinai—
Monastic and Marine

The coastline of the Sinai Peninsula, jutting south like an inverted pyramid with the Gulf of Suez on the west and the Gulf of Aqaba on the east, is very different from the Red Sea of the mainland. Access to the sea is via the relatively few key resorts, which, over the past quarter of a century, have created their own identities.

I first visited Sharm al-Sheikh in 1988. At that time, there were only two hotels on Na'ama Bay, one of which was barely more than a series of beach huts. My friend and I snorkeled, surrounded by incredible marine life of all sizes, shapes, and colors. From the beach, the sea had looked flat and dark, surrounded by featureless coast; under the water it was a new universe.

In those days, I would take the overnight bus to Sharm and get dropped off at first light by the side of the road. Sometimes I was literally the only person in the bay, but I did not realize then that I was seeing the beginning of the end for those reefs and fish. Over the coming years, hotels and resorts proliferated, driving the diving experience farther out and turning Sharm al-Sheikh into a town of all-you-can-eat buffets for tens of thousands of tourists a year.

Today you need to go to more characterful resorts to find the kind of holiday I enjoyed in the eighties. In Dahab, for instance, you can set your own agenda for the day and either do absolutely nothing in a laid-back atmosphere or explore some of the most outstanding reefs and dive holes on the planet at affordable prices. All that coupled with a bouncy, sometimes noisy nightlife that makes everyone feel young. In both directions from Dahab are multiple resorts, which focus

An early-morning diving lesson for beginners

on the relaxed-getaway type of tourism delivered by beautiful scenery and a limitless horizon of water and beach.

Dahab is just a short drive or taxi ride out of Sharm al-Sheikh, but the journey there really helps you understand that the Sinai is a unique region with a landscape and desert distinct from the North African deserts of mainland Egypt. The towering mountains and escarpments flanking the twisting roads are shot through with layers of color that catch the light of early morning and late afternoon. When the sun is overhead, you can feel very far away from humankind as you

The Neptune Hotel, like many in Dahab, provides a simple, clean, value-for-money holiday. It also has the best view of the bay from its breakfast terrace.

The many restaurants along Dahab's strip compete for business with unusual décor

go down roads that seem never-ending in the shimmering, sometimes brutal heat.

It is easy to imagine yourself back in a time when these roads were the tracks of the Bedouin who roamed the region, and who still seem to own the area. Even today their knowledge is vital if you want to get off the beaten track in this zone, which has a sensitive security situation due to its strategic location between several countries.

Driving along the road to Dahab, your excitement builds as you glimpse the sea to your right. The line where sea and

sky meet only becomes apparent as the road levels out and the sequence of resorts, roadside cafés, and buildings appears.

Dahab as a region can be divided into three main areas. Masbat, which includes the Bedouin village Asalah, is in the north and is fairly well developed, with many camps and hostels. Traveling south of Masbat brings you to Mashraba, which is more touristic and has considerably more hotels. This is where the road from Sharm al-Sheikh arrives. Finally, there is the Medina area, which lies to the southwest and includes

Dahab's sea front offers wonderful views, food, drink, and fun times from morning till night

the famous Laguna stretch of coast, frequently visited for its excellent shallow-water windsurfing.

The budget hotels that pepper the Dahab seafront are simple, but are generally clean and provide a place to recover from what may have been both a busy day in the sea and a busy night in the bar. The Dahab day starts early for those who are diving and quite late for everyone else.

The many cafés and bars lining the seafront provide a seemingly infinite choice of laid-back spots in which to enjoy

an Inside Out experience like nowhere else in Egypt. During the day, the slow pace of life enables you to sit overlooking the bay, drinking coffee or a beer, while reading, writing, enjoying time with friends, or simply watching life go by.

If you are feeling energetic and eager for some history and culture, the journey to Saint Catherine's Monastery, in the mountains in the middle of the peninsula, is another memorable drive. Depending on the car, you can enjoy air-conditioned comfort or open windows blasting you with hot air as you speed along. Either way, the views vary from spectacularly convoluted landscapes to long, straight roads. The drive from Dahab takes two and a half hours and may include a multitude of security points, which partly dictate the route taken. However, the drivers are usually Bedouin and on any given day will know the preferred route.

Visiting Saint Catherine's and climbing Mount Sinai is always a thrill. If ever there was a place where devotion to God entailed all the hardship that goes with establishing a monastery in the middle of nowhere, then this is it. Saint

A morning of diving along Dahab's world-famous reefs lies ahead for these visitors

Catherine's Monastery (officially the "Sacred Monastery of the God-Trodden Mount Sinai") sits at the mouth of a gorge at the foot of Mount Sinai. It was built in the middle of the sixth century and is one of the oldest working Christian monasteries in the world. Built by order of Emperor Justinian (r. 527–65), it encloses the Chapel of the Burning Bush, supposedly built on the site where Moses received the Ten Commandments. With such major biblical events as its background, it is easy to see why pilgrims have journeyed from all corners of the globe to experience living religious history.

The site, its history and jaw-dropping location aside, remains a working monastery and contains the world's oldest continuously operating library. The library possesses many unique books, including twelve pages and other fragments from the renowned fourth-century Codex Sinaiticus. This, along with over 3,300 other manuscripts, form the world's oldest and most important Christian monastic library. Around two-thirds of the texts are in Greek; other languages represented include Arabic, Syriac, Georgian, Hebrew, Polish, Ethiopic, Armenian, Latin, and Persian. Most of the

A short cycle ride from Dahab's waterfront takes you to quiet beaches and space to meditate

manuscripts are Christian texts for use in the services, or to inspire and guide the monks in their dedication. However, many are of an educational nature, such as classical Greek texts, lexicons, medical texts, and travel accounts.

For many, the highlight of a visit to this area is climbing Mount Catherine in the early morning to see the sunrise from the peak. This is the highest point of the Sinai peninsula, reaching a height of 2,646 meters. You should join up with others who are climbing that day to begin the ascent from the Chapel of the Forty Martyrs, from where it takes around

four hours to reach the summit. The peak itself is surmounted by the Chapel of Saint Catherine, which is adjoined by two small rooms and a kitchen area for pilgrims. From the summit, looking north, it is possible to see the Red Sea and the distant mountains of mainland Egypt. I remember vividly the first time I climbed this mountain with a friend. We were determined young guys and, wanting to be the first to the peak, we set off earlier than everyone else. It was cool and fresh in winter and thirty years ago I was fit enough to climb the height with ease. The predawn light showed the distant horizons and

Despite the solitude of Saint Catherine's Monastery there is life all around it

(though this was perhaps my imagination) the very curve of the earth. The silence was only broken as we came around the last corner to find a German choir singing into the sunrise ... they had slept on the summit all night. It was truly magical to experience this musical devotion in such a holy place.

All around the monastery itself and across the region as a whole you will see the local Bedouin, who exist side by side with the local security forces in what for them is their homeland. The term Bedouin in Arabic refers to one who lives out in the open, in the desert. The story goes that when Justinian built the monastery, he brought around two hundred families from Anatolia and Alexandria to guard it and defend the monks and those living in Saint Catherine's. The Bedouin today see themselves as the descendants of that first group, and are well aware of and proud of their Greek and Roman heritage. Thus, even though they converted to Islam in the seventh century, they remain true to their vows to defend the monastery.

Another option if you want to experience the Red Sea is to head to the coast that is the eastern border of mainland Egypt.

Saint Catherine's Monastery, looking Outside In

Eating by the marina in El Gouna brings
fine food and new friends

The Red Sea's riches provide
inspiration and color

El Gouna is one of the world's premier destinations for kite surfing and other water sports

FOLLOWING PAGES: Sharm al-Sheikh,
where you find the strangest things in the
local parking lot!

The beach in Hurghada provides a more leisurely holiday. A day of tourists, swimming, and selfies lies ahead.

With resorts running south from Ain Sukhna for hundreds of miles, there are choices of price and style to suit every budget. Of course, the Inside Out is from shore to sea, but there are many activities to enjoy, as well as simply lying in the sun by sea or pool. The more upmarket resorts are mostly newer, such as El Gouna, which has almost the feel of a small separate world and benefits from highly controlled traffic and the accompanying tranquility. Super-yachts abound, as do wonderful windy beaches that attract water-sports enthusiasts from across the world. Parties run late and the day begins slowly along the Red Sea. Because the coast is just a few hours from Cairo, the routes from the capital fill on Fridays, especially with those taking a quick dip around Ain Sukhna. Down toward Marsa Allam there are more places to really get away from it all, which means mentally leaving Egypt to play in golf tournaments or pretend you are on the Côte d'Azur. Hurghada is by far the largest resort on the mainland side, and suffers in some areas from overuse.

The Red Sea at sunrise

However, there are still wonderful beaches and warm waters in the more secluded resorts, especially south of the city, and even the most introverted visitor can find a spot to lie in peace and recharge tired batteries.

If you seek some history along the coast, a visit to Quseir is highly recommended. In former days, this was a rich port that exported wheat and was a key transit point for pilgrims to Mecca. The remains of the fort, some beguiling back streets, and a lighthouse make it worth a visit. Always quiet, it has a small beach, which feels like a genuinely historic spot. Sipping a coffee on the beach at Quseir provides a little moment of magical downtime.

Lagoon life in El Gouna, Inside Out

Looking out from shade and trees to sun and seas. El Gouna is pure escapism.